NO HERO, I CONFESS

NO HERO, I CONFESS

A Nineteenth-Century Autobiography

Edited by Margaret P. Medlicott

TAPLINGER PUBLISHING COMPANY
NEW YORK

First published in the United States in 1970 by
TAPLINGER PUBLISHING CO., INC.
29 East Tenth Street
New York, New York 10003

SBN 8008-5590-6
Library of Congress Catalog Number 75-103016

Printed in Great Britain

To
NORTON

And I, what I seem to my friend, you see:
What I soon shall seem to his love, you guess:
What I seem to myself, do you ask of me?
No hero, I confess.

ROBERT BROWNING

FOREWORD

My great-grandfather, Christopher Norton Wright, bookseller and publisher of Long Row, Nottingham, began to write his life story in 1813, when he was twenty-three years old. His last entry, made in 1871, completed a full-length autobiography and the whole work was contained in a stack of notebooks packed with fine, close writing.

Christopher's eldest son, Norton, who promised to edit the work after his father's death, never attempted it, implying to the rest of the family that the task was beyond him and that he would leave his own children to tackle it. I believe that his true reason was concern for the feelings of Christopher's fourth and surviving wife, Anne, who was sincerely loved by all the family and who, after many years of happy marriage, was still a little jealous of her predecessors.

The notebooks lay unexplored in their original wrappings until a few years ago when they and the family portraits reached my brother, the last of the line. He passed the notebooks to me and when I unpacked them to begin this work, I found in the last and thickest the heirloom gold watch-chain, which after Christopher's death caused some concern by its disappearance. Attached to it was a piece of paper reading: "For my descendant who reads as far as this, with my love, C.N.W.'

Although I believe he knew that Norton would not edit his life story, I doubt if he imagined the watch-chain would lie undiscovered for nearly a century.

CHAPTER I

Born on the 6th March, 1790, the author of this autobiography thinks that when he is at rest with his fathers, his dear children may be interested in knowing the events of his somewhat chequered life.

I write for their amusement and perhaps in some things they may also be instructed.

To begin in the usual way with some account of my ancestors, as far as my knowledge goes: – my grandfather, Samuel Wright, married Ann, daughter of Robert Chandler, of Tamworth in Staffordshire. They were what the world calls well-to-do and when I was born my grandfather had a large property at Drayton, on the same spot where now stands the Manor House of Sir Robert Peel.

My grandfather also had a mill at Fazeley, which has long since been pulled down. He was a very rich man until he unfortunately became acquainted with Lord Chancellor Thurlow, in consequence of a contested election for Tamworth. My grandfather espoused his cause and kept open house, extravagantly entertaining the first families in the county, with the result that he much impaired his estate. Unwise speculation reduced it still further and my father, who had started life as a rich man's son was, as this history will prove, ill-trained to make his living.

My mother was Caroline Elisabeth, only daughter of Sir Fletcher and Lady Norton. Before her marriage she frequented the assemblies at Tamworth, was considered a rich heiress, and was toasted for her beauty and charm as The Rose of Fazeley. However, when she met my father it was love at first sight and although she was offered fortunes she refused them all and ran away with him, contracting a hasty and secret marriage, but he had no money, her father would not forgive and so they parted for a time; she taking refuge with a relative; he to live in poor lodgings.

Then, disconsolate and longing for his society, she returned to him and they both went to Birmingham, where he obtained a situation, although only as a journeyman. He has told me that he often worked until eight in the evening, walked the fifteen miles home (and back in the morning, about thirty miles a day) but he was well-rewarded with the most kind and affectionate of wives.

At the end of a year their first child, Elizabeth, was born. Then came the fruits of poverty. My mother, brought up as a lady in the greatest luxury and having no-one to whom she could impart her situation, could provide only the barest necessities for the young stranger. However, what will a mother not do for her children? Five more followed, and to all of us she was the fondest, the kindest the most affectionate of mothers. Thousands of instances rush to my mind of her care and fondness, particularly to me, not through any partiality, but because she judged me to be the most weakly. For two years they had no idea I could live. Night after night she obtained no rest, yet she never failed in care and fondness. At length I mended and became the most hearty child of the family.

As soon as I could speak she taught me that prayer to Our Father, which all my life has been the first and the last, morning and evening, and how many times when repeating it have I recalled the features of that best of mothers.

My earliest recollections begin with the death of my sister Elizabeth, who was drowned in the canal in the third year of her age. A servant met me in the fields, told me my sister was drowned, subdued my sobs, and taking me in her arms carried me to the school – a dame's school, as it was then called – where I remained until after the funeral. Elizabeth was buried in Tamworth churchyard in the angle on the right, a little distance from the principal entrance to the belfry.

The next memorable event happened while I was still in petticoats. I was bringing a quantity of shavings from the stable where a carpenter was at work. In stepping on the fender, I put my pinafore on the fire and was soon in a blaze myself. A servant heard me scream and running into the room, extinguished the flames. This was my first escape from death! I was then about five years old.

The next calamity was my falling into the canal, the particulars of which I do not recollect. I was taken out apparently dead.

A short time after this, while the Lock House was being repaired, a tile fell from the roof and pitched upon my head, cutting deeply into the scalp, the mark of which I shall carry to my grave.

Thus a third time did I escape death.

Some time afterwards, I was again taken out of the canal, though not in so much danger as before, as I was seen falling in and was quickly rescued.

When I was six years old, in consequence of seeing an iron ring, red-hot in the fire, I took it out with the poker. Unfortunately I lifted the poker too high and the red-hot ring slid down to my hand and burned it most dreadfully. I was a long time recovering from the injury.

During the summer of that year, while I was eating gooseberries in the garden, my brother Henry with whom I was playing said I had eaten more than my share and he would have them out again. Believing him to be serious, I ran away from him and in getting over a wall, I fell with my neck upon an iron scraper which lacerated my throat almost to my windpipe. It was sewn up by Dr Bird and the mark of it remains now. 'You young rascal' said the doctor, who knew my history, 'you have escaped the grave so many times you are evidently born to be hanged!'

I cried bitterly when I told my mother of this, but she

comforted me, assuring me that Dr Bird was jesting, and gave me a halfpenny, to spend as I would.

It was then I began to acquire my love of books, which has lasted all my life. With my halfpenny I went to Mr More's toyshop at Tamworth and purchased two farthing books and these, with some others, started me in my trade as a bookseller. The first penny book which I bought was entitled *The History of Miss Patty Proud*, which I still have in my library.

During my sixth year, my father removed to Fazeley, where he kept the White Lion which was then and is now, the principal inn of the place. Henry and I were sent to a school conducted by Mr Francis Hudson and his mother, at Coleshill, Tamworth, where we continued to receive instruction for some years.

During the year 1802 – when the Treaty of Amiens was confirmed – I decided that until I could become a real bookseller I must make money in other ways. I ran errands, weeded gardens, and read the Bible to a blind gentleman until I had enough cash to purchase a sheep off Mr Freeman, butcher of Drayton, which I carried away with me on horseback. It was roasted whole in the market place, then taken to a large room at the back of the White Lion, cut up and distributed to the villagers. For this I made no charge, using the occasion to increase our goodwill. This was the proudest moment of my life.

I then entered into partnership with Sam Webster, a boy of about my own age. We collected bones, old iron, wool from the hedges and a variety of other objects, until I had sufficient money to purchase an old repeater watch. I took it out and made it strike so often that at last it would not strike at all and was quite spoilt.

My father frequently visited Birmingham. On one of his journeys he bought for me a small poem entitled *The Orphan Boy*. This I soon learnt by heart and by repeating it to the company at The Lion, frequenting the parlour, I obtained sufficient money to purchase a live sheep which shortly produced two lambs one of which became rickety and died and the other of which I sold for eighteen shillings. With part of this money I purchased a tobacco box, on the top of which, in gilt letters, was the following inscription:

'A halfpenny pay before you fill
Or forfeit sixpence, which you will.'

As a perquisite for waiting upon the company, my father allowed me the profits.

I now became a regular dealer in tobacco, purchased of Mr Lloyd, a Quaker, of Dale End, Birmingham. This tobacco was neatly wrapped-up in penny squares; also round ounce and half-ounce packets, upon which were enigmas, maxims, etc., the novelty of which caused a very considerable sale.

Mr Joseph Peel was in the habit of using more tobacco in his pipe than any other and on all occasions, when he filled it, I was conscious of a financial loss. On one occasion he called me and said: 'Kit, see what a rose I have got.' This was a large quantity of tobacco at the top of the pipe which in lighting caused great waste. He had so often done this before that my patience was exhausted, especially as the action was accompanied by somewhat spiteful teasing, so that to my shame, when he had spoken I kicked his shins until they bled. The company said it served him right: he took it in good temper but never over-filled his pipe again.

(Thus I had the distinction of kicking the shins of the Uncle of the future Sir Robert Peel, Prime Minister.)

My mother was in the habit of sending me to old Charles Birch, the grocer, with 3s. 2d. to purchase a pound of tobacco. One day I went to another shop and asked what they would charge for a pound of tobacco and they said that if I came regularly it would be 3s. I bought a pound and pocketed the twopence, but alas for that twopence, my peace of mind was gone as my mother supposed it came from Birch's as usual and after the working of my conscience, I told all and gave her the twopence back. She said I had done very wrong in taking it, but as I had told her she forgave me and let me keep it and allowed me always to keep the twopence whenever I fetched tobacco again.

When I was about thirteen years old, I went to a boarding school at Barne, near Walsall, kept by Mr Mayne and his two sons. Be it said to my honour that this was done entirely out of my own savings, my having hoarded in an old stocking sixteen bright golden guineas! It was intended that I should be a surgeon and I was to be apprenticed to a Mr Richard Bird, who had brought me into the world. Of course I was to learn Latin, which I never could bear, and I used to bathe my forehead in cold water, thinking that as I cooled it, my brain would retain the lessons my master set me! I can well remember declining 'lapis, lapidis, lapidi' and as a stone was my poor brain at this time. However, those were happy days. We had a noggin of milk each morning; a good dinner to which we brought keen appetites, and in the evening those boys whose parents could send them bacon were allowed to toast a rasher in the kitchen. We went nearly two miles to church on Sunday and on the return walk, hungry as young tigers, we would begin to visualise the dinner which awaited us: the roast beef done to a turn, dripping its juices on to the potatoes in the pan, the Yorkshire pudding, the rich gravy and the fruit pie or pudding which followed. The eating of confectionery was not encouraged, but after dinner on Sunday each boy received, as a weekly treat, a handful of sugar-plums, a striped sugar-stick and a square of treacle toffee. These were supposed to last all the coming week, but few of these goodies survived beyond the Monday evening.

We had a beautiful playground on the green opposite the school, containing about two acres, now alas enclosed. On Wednesday and Saturday a travelling baker came from Birmingham with penny and twopenny custards. Of these

I devoured numbers and have never since tasted their like, as the custard was made from new-laid eggs and fresh, full-cream milk.

On November fifth, some of the elder boys made an effigy of our old master, Mr Mayne, and after parading him round the green, his pockets well-filled with serpents, crackers, etc., he was set alight and blown up, among the shouts of nearly all the boys. One of the elder boys, the ringleader, was flogged and expelled from the school. I nearly met with this fate myself, from the following trick:

I had been to visit my dear grandparents at Coleshunt Wood. They sent their man, John Ditchfield, for me with a horse – not one of the fastest – and when at length we arrived I said I would have to start back half an hour earlier, riding behind John on this slow beast. The dear old lady, my grandmother, found me a large brass cooking pin which she put through one of my shoe-heels, for use as a spur. John would not allow me to use it, but I thought nevertheless it would give me some sport. One morning I put it through my shoe and when I went up to the master, I occasionally gave a gentle prick into the legs or ankles of the lads. Various 'Ohs!' and jerkings took place and at last I whipped it into the calf of a fat lad who roared most lustily. The master was in a great wrath and I expected either a flogging, a task, or both, but upon seeing the trick he joined the lads in hearty laughter. However, I put away my pin and had it by me for more than twenty years in a little box with other playthings of schoolboy happy hours.

Some time afterwards, I heard that my father was about to leave Fazeby for Hurstpierpoint, a village about seven miles from Brighton and that it was their intention to leave me at school. This preyed on my mind so that early one morning I ran away from school. It was a clear, bright frosty morning and when in the middle of Sutton Coldfield, I was so impressed with remorse at what I then considered the wickedness of my action, that I went down on my knees on the Heath and prayed to be forgiven and for a long time pondered whether I should return or go on. Making sure that a flogging awaited me in either case, but the shame of meeting my schoolfellows would be the worse, I went onwards and arrived at Fazeby at about 11 o'clock, finding to my dismay that my father had started for Birmingham early that morning, intending to call at Barne to see me on his way back! My mother hastened with me to my grandparents' house and very quickly the old horse was saddled, and mounted behind John, I was sent back to school, bearing with me, however, a letter from my mother, saying that Mr Mayne was not to chastise me as I had no other cause for leaving school than fear of being left behind. I arrived at school by 2 o'clock and while taking some refreshment in the kitchen, about ten minutes after my arrival my worthy sire trotted into the yard. Mr Mayne, who had been particularly requested not to mention my morning's ramble, said: 'Christopher, go into the school and I will in a short time call you to see your father.' This he did, and I went to see my father as though nothing had happened.

My father stayed for tea and the days being short agreed to stay the night. I asked as a great favour that I might be allowed to sleep with him which was granted and during the night I persuaded him to take me home in the morning to see my mother and brothers and my sister and bid them Goodbye before they left for Hurst. As it was but ten days before the holidays, he granted my wish. Accordingly, in the morning I went to the school for my clothes and announced to the boys that I was the Stag, the name by which the first boy going home was called. No allusion was made to my runaway adventure of the previous morning and they all shook hands and cheered me, with their heartiest wishes for enjoyment during the holidays.

A Mr Gorton conveyed all the family in a light waggon to Coventry where my father engaged the whole of the inside of a coach to convey us to London. The next day we were taken to lodgings in Westminster Road, where we stopped some weeks until the house was ready at Hurst.

Having much time to spare in London, I wandered up and down the streets and became acquainted with a lot of boys of my own age, I am sorry to say not of the most respectable kind. Among other exploits, we were in the habit of waiting at the door of the Surrey Theatre, begging ticket counterfoils of people leaving. The attempts to enter with these tickets were futile and the response was 'Get out, you vagabonds, or you shall be horsewhipped.' After many attempts to pass in this way my curiosity overcame my discretion and one evening, about an hour before the theatre opened to the public, I ran up the staircase into the gallery, having concocted a tale in case of meeting any of the parties of the theatre. Luckily (as I then thought) I met no-one and rapidly going over the seats I fixed myself in the very centre of the front row and laid myself at length on the seat. Very soon after I heard a person stepping from the top of the gallery to kindle the lights. My heart beat pit-a-pat and thump-thump, but this suspense was soon ended by an angry roar: 'What the D—— have we here?' followed by divers thumps and bangs on my person so that I called out 'Murder'.

I was hauled down and handed upon the stage, to undergo the operation of horsewhipping upon an improved principle, as there were four of the Masters of the Riding School, preparing to operate upon various parts of my body. My fright and cries were piteous. At length I offered my concocted story: 'Oh, don't flog me, for if you should hurt me, I shall not be able to lead my poor blind father who is a fiddler, about the streets of London.' This tale, with my apparent distress, so worked upon the feelings of my persecutors that they said 'Let us forgive him this time and let the poor fellow stop and see the performance.'

After about two months we removed by coach to Hurstpierpoint. The house was situated in the middle of the village, on the left-hand side from the Stone Pound Gate. A week after our arrival, the clergymen, the surgeon and some of the principal inhabitants sent messengers to say they would do themselves the pleasure of taking tea with us, naming the day, which I well remember was thought rather curious by my parents, but which we found was the customary way of greeting strangers on their arrival.

It was my father's intention to open a boarding- and day-school, the premises being very large and well-calculated for such a purpose. Here some of the happiest hours of my life were passed as there was a large lawn, bowling-green, fishpond and kitchen garden well-stocked with fruit trees, among which were some of the finest fig-trees I have ever seen. From the lawn there was an extensive view of the Downs and on stormy nights the roar of the sea could be distinctly heard.

My father advertised the terms of his school in the London and country newspapers and had a copperplate note struck off in exact imitation of a £50 Bank of England note, with the words, in large lettering, '50 miles from London.'

On the long-anticipated morning of the school's opening, we were all anxiously expecting a number of boarders, but by the close of day only one had made his appearance! This, with about half-a-dozen day scholars was all my father had to commence with, nor had he much increase during the half-year, after which time this speculation was given up with a loss of about £500.

We afterwards found out that a French boy (who my father had exchanged at Dieppe for my brother John, each to be educated abroad for seven years) had raised injurious reports of my father in regard to his having kept an inn before he went to Hurst. This, though certainly true, made no shame to my father but was much against the success of his undertaking.

Among other forms of recreation, my father adopted certain scientific pursuits. He acquired a powerful electrifying machine and frequently gave shocks to parties suffering from various complaints. In this respect he was highly successful and told me privately that he had vowed to himself to work a cure on an old woman who could scarcely walk for rheumatism in her hip joints. 'I will make her move' he said to me 'and I have a plan in which I shall need your help: but do not tell your mother of it, for she would not approve.'

I was ordered to get a jug of warm water and at the moment of the shock quietly to pour some behind the old woman. My father said: 'Bless my soul,' ma'am, the shock seems to have upset you' and she, beholding the steamy pool, cried 'Oh, sir; I beg ten thousand pardons' and prepared to mop it up with her handkerchief.

'Never mind,' said my father, and bid me fetch a cloth. The old lady, cured of her stiff joints, scampered off as quickly as possible and I will say now, that she was never so lame again. My father expressed the opinion to me, in private, that in such a case the end justified the means.

After leaving Hurst, my father took the Crown Inn, at Croydon. It was arranged that I should be apprenticed to Mr Richard Baker, Clock- and Watch-maker, Market Street, Tamworth, the agreed premium being fifty pounds. My mother accompanied me to London from whence we travelled by coach to Coventry, where we arrived at 4 o'clock on a fine summer's morning. My mother and I walked by the canal side for about half-a-mile to the house of one of my father's friends, with whom we breakfasted.

Being always fond of bathing, I stripped and jumped into the canal just below a lock, and thinking myself a better swimmer than I really was, endeavoured to reach the lock gates. This I achieved, but was exhausted, and in trying to take hold of the gate I slipped heels over head and should thus have finished the chapter, if some boatmen had not rescued me.

They took me out and laid me in their craft, insensible. A number of persons crowded around me, supposing I was dead, and they were joined by my mother who cried 'Oh my son; my poor son is drowned!'

I soon recovered – my third escape from a watery grave – and after a severe lecture from my mother we returned to our lodging.

After a few days, I was duly bound apprentice to Mr Baker, my mother returning to Croydon, and my first job was to make brass watch pins, some thousand of which I manufactured. I progressed and was fond of my trade, although my life with Mr Baker was not easy, he thinking nothing of cuffing me about the head and ears if he thought me somewhat slow in mastering a new process which needed careful application. However, in about two months I became so proficient that in one day alone I earned my master one guinea by clock-cleaning.

About this time the Volunteers were called up for a short period of training and I had a great number of firelocks to clean, the operation of which was to place them in a vice and polish them with fine sandpaper, afterwards cleaning the inside with herbs fixed on the ramrod. The month being October, there was among other weapons sent for cleaning, a valuable fowling piece. Not having had such a one before and supposing the bronze of the barrel to be rusty, I placed it in the vice and stripping off my coat, prepared to operate upon it with sandpaper of the roughest type. After about two hours' hard labour, I made it as bright and shining as a looking-glass, and while I was admiring my handiwork my master came in and seeing what I had done, without any explanation unscrewed the vice, took hold of the gun and with a countenance distorted with rage shouted, 'I'll try the temperature of this gun on your skull and see which is the harder!' He then dealt me a blow with the barrel which indeed proved the thickness of my skull, for it was saved by Providence from damage. I thought he had gone raving mad, as he had never explained to me the difference between a sportsman's fowling piece and the bright gun of the Infantry soldier.

Upon the impulse of the moment, I snatched up a basin of dirty water and threw it and its contents at my master's head as a further experiment on the relative thickness of skulls, then, not waiting to see the result, I ran outside and up Castle Hill, which adjoined. This being very steep and he being very fat, he could not well follow me and to add to his ire I kept laughing and taunting him, shouting that he should never see me again.

I hovered about until the coast was clear, then I ran upstairs, secured my small stock of clothes and 2s. 6d. in money – all my worldly wealth – and ran away from a hardhearted and cruel master.

I set off for Coleshill, a distance of about ten miles, during which journey I ran, expecting every moment that some person would be sent after me. However, no-one followed. I occasionally paused to consider the step I had taken and bitterly regretted it. Had my master been of a more kindly disposition I certainly would have returned, as nothing can extenuate the crime (without great provocation) of running away from an apprenticeship, such recklessness branding the party in after-life as a vagabond and wastrel. I am happy to say, however, that such was not the case with me, as my after-life will show.

I entered a small pothouse in Coleshill and changed my half-crown for a halfpennyworth of beer and a pennyworth of bread and cheese. In a few minutes, observing my fatigue and uneasiness, the landlord said: 'My lad, you've run away from your apprenticeship.' As a verification of his suspicions, I instantly ran out of the house and fled through Coleshill. About three miles farther on was a large reservoir and thinking I was now out of the way of pursuers, I rested myself and when cool enough, stripped and swam a considerable distance into the water where I found a night fishing line with a large pike, both of which I captured and brought to shore. This prize procured for me a few shillings at a roadside Public House. I pushed on to Stonebridge, Hampton and Knowle, where I proceeded by the canal side to Coleshunt Wood, the residence of my grand-parents. They were both very glad to see me and I told them I had a holiday from my master. My grandfather went to bed first, after which I told my grandmother that I had run away and was desperate to know what to do. We had a hearty cry together and she insisted on giving me a half-sovereign, with her prayers that I would come to no harm. I kissed her fondly and bade her goodnight.

I slept very little, under the constant dread of pursuit, and at 3 o'clock in the morning left the safety of my grandparents' home to encounter the mazes of a troublesome world. My road lay through the romantic scene of Kenilworth and in spite of my anxiety I enjoyed the morning's walk, arriving in due course at the ancient city of Coventry. My fears of capture had not left me, therefore I hastened on, tired out in mind and body.

I entered a spacious inn yard and seating myself upon a stone horse block, thought how happy I would be if, like Whittington of old, I could hear the Tamworth bells ring 'Turn again—' After sitting on the horse block for a time, I espied a large stone trough, full of clear water. Being footsore and dusty, and without considering the possible consequences, I pulled off my shoes and forthwith entered this bath. While in the act of washing the dust from my blistered feet I heard a rough voice say: 'You young scamp! What are you doing here?' Then applying a Hurculean hand, the owner of the voice continued: 'As you have washed your feet for your own pleasure you shall have your head washed for mine' and I was soused over head and ears with water. All this was observed by a rubicund coach guard, who said, 'Perhaps the poor lad can't read.'

Over the trough, in legible letters was printed:

'He who fouls this water clear
Shall sixpence pay in ale or beer.'

This I had not noticed. The good-natured coach guard paid the sixpence for me and took me into the inn kitchen; then asked me where I came from. I told him all my tale and he said, 'Well, my lad, I'll give you a ride to London for nothing.' This seemed too good to be true, but alas! how evanascent are momentary enjoyments. I had a penny loaf in my pocket and seeing a large piece of beef roasting, I divided my loaf in two, sharpened a piece of stick lying in the hearth and having toasted the bread, soused it in the dripping-pan. Having eaten this with great relish, I began to operate on the other half and had got so far as its immersion in the dripping-pan when the cross-grained cook, seeing what was going on, dabbed the remainder of the greasy loaf about my ears. However, I did not mind this much. Having my belly nearly full and the promise of a ride to London, I was comparatively happy, knowing that if I could see my mother, all would be well.

I was out all night and sat by the guard who was particularly interested in my adventure and treated me to refreshment on the way to London where I arrived at about 3 o'clock in the morning. My Good Samaritan, the guard, affectionately bade me goodbye and I parted with him regretfully. He must have been dead long ago, but his kindness to me will be remembered with gratitude while I live.

I had recollected that in some of my mother's letters she had mentioned a fishmonger of Croydon, named Page, who attended Billingsgate Market daily, for the purpose of retailing at Croydon. I thought I might find him at Billingsgate, to which place I hied my way and arrived at about 4 o'clock.

The first thing I saw was two Billingsgate fishwomen, fighting, one of whom being worsted in the battle, seized a large fish by the tail, slapped it in her adversary's face and shouted 'Take that, you Brimstone!' The other in her turn seized a large fish from her basket and the battle became extremely interesting to the onlookers. At length the women closed upon each other and rolling in the mud, each with her habiliments torn by the other's frenzy, were separated by a constable of the Market, Sir Robert Peel's policemen not then being in existence.

My first inquiry for Mr Page was at a gin shop, and asking the landlord if he knew of that name, he said 'Oh, my good lad, there he sits', and turning round, I found a red face and burly person looking like John Bull, smoking his pipe with a glass before him. I soon told him my tale, asked him about my parents and found he knew them well. I asked him to allow me to ride in his fish cart to Croydon, to which he at once consented, and having provided myself with a penny roll and butter, I took my departure from London. I never enjoyed shrimps and bread and butter more in my life than I did that morning, as the kind fishmonger allowed me as many shrimps as I liked.

We reached Croydon at about 7 o'clock and Mr Page, while supplying my mother with fish, told her he had brought her son Christopher to Croydon. Soon I was indoors, relating my adventures to her. At the conclusion she said she would take the best opportunity to inform my father but had no hopes of his forgiveness and begged most earnestly that I kept out of his sight as she dreaded the consequences. She gave me a good supper and sent me to sleep in the attic.

By the next day's post my father received a letter of a most insulting nature from Mr Baker, the purport of which was that if my father harboured me he should consider the father as bad as the son and he would have nothing further to do with either of us. This letter was so offensive to my father's feelings that he said 'Carrie, you know something of this affair. Where is the lad? I am not surprised at his running away from such a brute of a master: if he is in Croydon send for him that I may know about it.'

My mother, although much pleased, said nothing at the time but after my father had gone for the day she sent me to the Crown Inn. I went with fear and trembling but had a better reception than I anticipated, and after I had related all the circumstances my father said 'Your master is a brute and I'll make him repay the fifty pounds I paid for you.'

After various legal threats, Mr Baker said he would overlook past offences and would be glad to receive the lad back again. My father would not hear of it and said I might be tap-boy at the Crown. The substance of this situation was to go for errands, clean knives and forks, boots and shoes and carry out pots of beer for dinner and supper to about fifty customers. A most wearisome life I led for about two months.

It might have continued longer, if I had not one day chanced to say to my mother, 'Has my father ordered the hay rick to be thatched?'

'No', she said, 'but I have asked him many times to get it done.'

'You may ask him many more times, but the rick will be spoiled before it is done.'

I was unaware that my father stood behind me at the time and heard what I said to my mother. 'So that is your opinion of me, young gentleman, is it?' he thundered, and seizing a very thick stick he struck me with great force. My mother flew between us: 'Henry, you'll kill the lad. If you strike again you'll strike me!'

Of course I escaped from the house as soon as possible. In a few days my mother obtained for me a situation as shop boy to a linen draper named Armstrong, of 222 High Street, in The Borough, at ten guineas a year with all my board and lodging. I was very hardworked but had plenty of grub, cheerful companions in the shop and my time passed pleasantly away.

Among other avocations I had to go every day to my master's bank in Lombard Street and once, in passing over London Bridge, I had the misfortune to lose a cheque. My master was very angry, suspecting my honesty, and to discover the truth made the following test. While I was gone on an errand, he made a cheque similar to the one I had lost and for the same amount and having dropped it into a position where I was sure to see it when I returned, stood out of sight to watch the effect when I perceived it. When I entered the shop I soon found what I supposed to be the original cheque and shouted at the top of my voice to my companions, 'Hurrah, lads! Now master will know I am not a thief; here is the cheque; I must have dropped it before I left the shop.' He came downstairs directly and said 'Well, my lad, I am very sorry I suspected your honesty but I am now satisfied that you did lose it as I drew this one to imitate the original and to test you.'

About this time my master began to court the daughter of the landlord of the Spurr Inn, in the Borough, and frequently returned home late at night. On one occasion, his sister who kept house for him was engaged in bottling some gin from a small cask. When filling the bottles instead of pouring out sufficient gin to insert the cork, she would put each one to her mouth, thinking the quantity but a small one, and kept sipping until there was room to insert the cork. After half-an-hour the effect of these potations was apparent from the brightness of her eyes and the volubility of her tongue, and at length she became completely intoxicated. Knowing the temper of her brother, I decided that I must get her to bed, and I carried her upstairs, although with great difficulty. While endeavouring to make her comfortable, I was horrified to find her arms suddenly close about my neck, almost strangling me, while she poured forth in my unwilling ear protestations of passion. Hot with shame I tried to struggle free, but the more I tried, so much the more did she cling and invite me, as she said, to prove my manhood upon her.

Considerably frightened (I was but thirteen years old, although being well-grown I looked somewhat older) I managed eventually to free myself and then left her, going downstairs and putting all away, that my master might not know what had happened. In the morning I got up very early, made the fires and got breakfast ready and did all I could, saying Missus was very poorly and could not get up. In a few days' time, in her brother's absence she again became intoxicated and at last it happened so frequently that I could no longer hide it from him. She promised him to abstain from gin, but all to no purpose. Several weeks later, Mr Armstrong brought home his bride and his sister was made to leave. I much regret to say it was afterwards related to me that she took to a life of shame.

How easy it is for one vice to breed others and how weak is human nature! Should we not all seek constant guidance from above, to strengthen our characters and evade the Tempter?

Two of the young men who were both considered clever in the shop, occasionally rang the changes on the customers in the following way. When a lady demanded the best Irish linen and then attempted to knock down the proper price, one of the men would be prepared with a piece somewhat coarser and the second man would divert the lady's attention while, as quickly as lightning, the two pieces would change hands. A piece of linen upon which the usual fair profit would be obtained was wrapped-up before the lady, she supposing she had made a great bargain. This was never done when the customer acted fairly.

CHAPTER 2

After remaining about thirteen months in this situation, I left, having received ten guineas wages. I then obtained a place with Mr Cowlan, a Linen Draper opposite St George's Church, the Borough, where I stayed only six weeks and where I was cheated out of the whole of my previous year's wages. We were supplied every morning with coffee and hot rolls for breakfast and the young men in the shop – finding I had this money – commandeered my share of the rolls each day and made me toss for them with pence. As no other food was available until 2 o'clock dinner, I bought my rolls dearly, as from pence we got to shillings and half-crowns until I had lost all my money. I was afraid to mention this to my master, as I was threatened with dire consequences.

After leaving Mr. Cowlan, I returned to the Crown Inn, Croydon, and for a short time resumed my labours as pot boy. This was in 1804, at the time when the Wandsworth and Merstham Railway was in course of formation, being the first public railway to be constructed in the United Kingdom. A Mr Edward Banks was the principal agent, having brought a number of engineers from Butterly Park, Derbyshire. Many a hundred gallons of porter I took to these men while they were working on the line.

Shortly afterwards, I took a liking to a Mr Andrews, a wholesale and retail grocer, who bought large quantities of damaged articles from the Customs House. The first day of my employment my (as I then thought) kind master set me to pick raisins and said to me 'Eat what you like, my lad: I always like my boys to enjoy themselves.'

After a while my occupation was changed to mixing oatmeal with figs that had been damaged by overheating. This was a change of luxury and of course I ate some of the finest. At one o'clock on that first day I went in to dinner but in consequence of my over-indulgence in sweets, I had no appetite. In the afternoon I resumed my occupation and continued the surfeit of the morning, until finding in the figs many grubs which the oatmeal was intended to disguise, I became very sick and to this day I have never touched figs again. I found afterwards that this was always done by my shrewd master to cause a surfeit so that the boys might not always be pilfering.

I was so ill that I was obliged to go to bed, but the next day was as well as ever and at dinner ate very heartily of boiled rice and treacle. This did very well for a few days but I discovered that this was called rough filling, the intention being that the boys and young men might not want much afterwards, and this would have been well if the treacle and rice had been of good quality, but both were damaged articles. At supper there was nothing but bread and Dutch cheese. I was growing very fast at the time and needed better and more liberal fare, but it was useless to complain. We had to work very hard, but this would have been of no account if we had not always been hungry.

One memorable day the affair was settled for me. We were unloading a number of Dutch cheeses. It was usual to throw from one to the other and my master's son would occasionally pretend to throw and not do so, then as I was ready to catch he would throw the cheese at my head. On that morning I bore this some half-dozen times, then I took up a cheese, threw it at his head, knocked him down, ran upstairs, procured my small bundle of clothes, got out of the window and, sliding down the roof, escaped from treacle, rice, figs and Dutch cheese for ever.

I decided to return to London, but having no money for coach hire, I set off to walk. The next day I arrived in

London, penniless and almost tired out. I slept in a cellar in Westminster Road and in the morning found my cash in hand amounted to one shilling. All my possessions were tied in a handkerchief. At 9 a.m. I began at the top of Ludgate Hill, asking at each draper's shop on both sides of the way if they wanted an errand boy. At a large drapers on the left side of Fleet Street next door to Messrs Laurie and Whittle, I entered and addressed myself to a fat good-natured-looking gent with powdered hair, silk stockings and a rubicund nose, asking my usual question, 'Please sir, do you want a shop boy?' Taking my worn-out hat from my head and thrusting me into a chair in the middle of the shop, he said, 'Sit there, my lad, and I'll teach you good manners.' After stepping to the door, with my hat in his hand, he turned, approached me with a low bow, and said: 'Pray, sir, are you in want of a shop boy?' He then returned my hat to my head, knocked it over my eyes, took me by the shoulder and said 'I hope this will teach you better manners when you enter a shop. Always pull off your hat to a gentleman'. Then putting his foot behind me he kicked me out of the shop, shouting 'You young rascal; you'll come to be hanged in the end.'

This incident made such a lasting impression on my mind that on this day it is as vivid as it was upon that awful moment.

Picking myself up, outside the shop, I burst into tears and sobbed so bitterly that I attracted the attention of passers-by. However, after walking up Fleet Street and the Strand I recovered myself, calling on my fortitude which I greatly needed: there was I, with one shilling in my pocket, all my wardrobe and possessions in a black silk handkerchief, a runaway apprentice, discarded by my father and my masters and without a character. My thoughts were not to be envied. However, on I trudged, calling at every draper as I passed, with my parrot-like question, 'Please sir, do you want a shop boy?' never again forgetting to take off my hat.

On I wandered, from Charing Cross, Pall Mall, Cockspur Street, Haymarket, Piccadilly, New and Old Bond Streets, when towards the top of the latter street, after the usual question, with hat in hand, pale, weary and dejected, I was told, 'Yes, I do, my lad. Have you a character from your last situation?' I answered, yet with doubt, that my former master, Mr Cowlan of High Street, the Borough, would give me one.

The gentleman said: 'I am going over the water this afternoon and will call on him. You may leave your bundle and come again at 9 in the morning.'

I had sixpence left from my shilling and this I laid out on a twopenny loaf, twopennyworth of cheese and, when night fell, a twopenny bed. I called punctually at nine o'clock the next morning. The gentleman said he had enquired and was told I had a good character when I lived there, but as I had stayed such a short time they supposed I had lost it. He then threw my bundle at me and said I had better go to sea, as he was afraid I was in a fair way for the Gallows.

Alone, friendless and penniless I paused irresolutely, not knowing how to act, then set forth on the long walk back to the City. There, near the Minories, I was taken on by a Mr Drake who, after enquiring about my character, said 'Well, my boy, go upstairs and get something to eat. We'll see about your character tomorrow.'

He did not pursue the matter and told me afterwards that he considered himself to be a good judge of character.

I was forthwith installed into one of the most hardy situations it was possible to imagine, at the astounding sum of eight guineas per annum. However, I was comparatively happy, having an empty pocket, ditto belly and little or no character. The following were my duties, during eighteen hours out of the twenty-four: I rose at six, made the house fires, opened shop, cleaned the boots and shoes for my master and six assistants, cleaned knives and forks and the shop windows and swept and dusted the shop. Between nine o'clock and ten, after all had breakfasted, I had the mincings for my share. I had then to assist the maid-servant in making the beds and emptying the slops, then I cleaned myself and from noon until five p.m. was constantly employed in errands. Then after a few scraps for dinner I had to assist in wrapping and straightening the drapery goods until midnight and sometimes one and two in the morning.

I was very anxious to give satisfaction and my master was so well pleased with me that after two months he said, 'Christopher, I shall raise your wages to ten guineas.' He added, 'As you have to be a year in the business of a draper you must know something of the trade.' On the following day I was instructed to stand on a stool outside the shop door and become a 'barker', the meaning of which was to shout to the passing crowd: 'Look here, my good women, large white handkerchiefs – twopence-halfpenny each – this is the cheapest shop in Ratcliffe Highway.' A crowd would soon gather and the assistants in the shop would be ready to serve the customers. My master found me so useful in this respect that he got another boy to do the household drudgery.

Then came an event which raised me much higher in this situation. I slept on a truckle bed under the counter, with one of the junior assistants. One night he woke me and in a trembling voice said: 'Hark, there are robbers in the shop.' In reply to this I muttered, 'Let us get out and cry "Murder!"' but he, between chattering teeth whispered, 'It is your place – you get out.'

Being in fear of having our throats cut if we lay, I said loudly: 'I'll fire my two pistols, you fire the guns in the direction where the thieves are and we are sure to kill one or two of them.' Then, making a great noise, I jumped out of bed and opening the front door – the thieves being at the back – I ran into the street shouting 'Thieves, Fire, Murder!' The watchman sprung his rattle, and the street was soon in an uproar. My master came down in his shirt and nightcap, half asleep and tipsy, with an old pistol in his hand. 'Where are the villains? Let them come on: this is how I'll serve them.' Then holding up both hands, he fired off the pistol and shot away the thumb of his left hand. In the meantime, the thieves, of whom there were two, were apprehended by the watch and a couple of sorry-looking villains they were.

A doctor attended to my master and after a few hours' rest he sent for me and said he should raise my wages to £20 a year and I should occupy the position of my cowardly companion, who was discharged.

After six months had passed, I received a letter from my father in Nottingham, where he was then living, to say that if I had sown my wild oats I might come to Nottingham to assist in his business. He had given up inn-keeping and had gone into partnership with a Mr Hall, an auctioneer.

I gave notice to Mr Drake and on 21st May, 1806, left London by the True Briton coach and after a ride of twenty-four hours reached the Black's Head Inn about the middle of the night. In the morning I made my way to the Auction Room. Here I had plenty to do, making up lots, writing lists and collecting bills. I still had time to spare and to amuse myself I read over my little stock of books from value one farthing to sixpence. The whole might have cost me two shillings. The idea occurred to me that if I could sell them I might be able to purchase others and so extend my stock of information. I then displayed a few in the window for which, having kept them quite clean, I found a ready sale, and I soon realised a capital of fifteen shillings.

I now turned my attention to attending the auctions, buying books, coins and other articles, employing my father to sell them of an evening, by which means, with strict economy, I soon realised £2. With my rapidly-increasing means I was able to start business seriously and on the next Saturday I borrowed two old trestles and having taken a door off the hinges for the day's use, I commenced business as a stall-keeper, returning the door each Saturday evening. Having added braces and blacking balls to my stock I became a tradesman, and was very proud of my position in society.

I became too independent for my situation with my father and took lodgings at one shilling a week with one of the most honest and amiable men that I ever met in my life. This kind old man was a bookseller in a small way and to add to my stock on a Saturday he usually lent me some books to add to the show of my own. I now – at not seventeen years old – became a commercial traveller in a small way. I purchased a box with leather straps and from Monday morning until Friday night I travelled the neighbouring villages, selling books, knives, scissors and braces. In January, 1807, I opened an account with Mr Charles Sutton, Bridlesmith Gate, and obtained from him considerable credit, thus extending my business. I purchased a regular stall and corner and for convenience to the market put my stall and stock in an empty stable in the passage next to the Queen's Head, at that time occupied by a Mr Clarke, Draper. However, after a few months, Mr Clarke quarrelled with my father and then seized all my stock in trade, stall, etc. and charged me £5 for rent, although he had given me leave to use the stable free of charge as he did not use it himself. This was a great misfortune to me as the money was equal to nearly all my effects in trade. I was, however, obliged to pay and when I did so, told him he was a villain, and that I should live to see him a pauper and an outcast and soon should be a better man than he was.

I then took a half shop, the other half being occupied by a shoemaker, at what I thought a great rent (£10 a year) and became a bookseller-stationer. I had learned somewhat from my own follies and was determined to succeed. Once, while reading the life of Dr Frankling who said that youth could vow to possess hereafter, by diligence and perseverance, anything that was attainable, I fixed my eyes on the principal house in the Market Place, then occupied by Orme and Hulse, Silversmiths, and said to myself: 'If I live, that house shall be mine.' This I accomplished, and sooner than I dreamed of.

I now, unfortunately, became acquainted with the Clerk of the Nottingham Race Course, who kept a billiards table in Bottle Lane. This I much frequented and often the earnings of a week would disappear in one way or another in a few hours. Eventually I was completely cured of my baneful propensities.

Having borrowed about £30, I started for London, to purchase goods for my new shop. On my first day of arrival, when passing along the Strand, I entered the wild beast show at Exeter Change. There I saw a door with 'Billiards' painted on it. I entered the room and began to play with a gent. We began with one shilling a game. I beat him easily; then we got to half-a-crown, and I still won. Then to crowns, and as I had won a considerable sum my antagonist pressed me to play for points. He allowed me to win one or two games. We then played double or quits and I occasionally won. Afterwards he gave me points until he gave me twenty-one out of twenty-four and he won until I had lost nearly all my £30. In an instant I thought what a fool I was, and leaving the table, renounced billiards and all gambling for ever.

After losing so much money, I dined off a penny loaf and then proceeded on my business. Seeing some books at what I thought were low prices at a pawnbroker's shop in High Holborn, I went in and laid out nearly all my remaining cash. I related my adventures to the proprietor, whose name I wish I could remember as he behaved in a most kind and gentlemanlike manner, and he said: 'I think I may have confidence in you, for you have an honest look: I will trust you for £50.' I took credit for a portion of that sum and by subsequent business, more than made up for my loss at billiards. I did business with this Good

Samaritan for many years – I hope and believe to his interest as well as my own.

After spending about ten days in London, I returned to my little snuggery, unpacked my treasures and prepared to be a bookseller in right earnest.

While in London I had made arrangements with Messrs. Taylor and Hessey, Booksellers in Fleet Street, to be my London correspondents, with which house I continued for a few years, and then entered into regular correspondence with Messrs Longman & Co. and Messrs Simpkin Marshall.

Shortly afterwards, an auction sale of books was conducted by Mr John Gaskell, at that time the most celebrated auctioneer in Nottingham. I attended the sale, exceeded the highest bid and purchased the whole lot for £20. This purchase was generally reported in the town: the bookworms of the day soon flocked to my shop and within a fortnight I had made a comfortable sum which far exceeded my outlay.

Being most concerned in establishing myself as a man of business and with the knowledge that I had no expectations of capital either now or hereafter from my family which, indeed, was a matter of conscience to me for I had constant thoughts of that dear mother whose mind was never at rest for the care of her children, all younger than myself, I had had little thought for the company and activities of young people like myself. Although I had learned some salutory lessons in relation to business, I was still unversed in the arch practices of young women, as I will now relate. However, I do not think I acquitted myself so foolishly as the beginning of this incident might suggest.

I was then lodging at a pleasant inn, the name of which I will omit. My landlord had a pretty daughter who took the greatest care of my comfort and seemed to have taken a fancy to me. As no likeness of me exists before my portrait was painted in my middle years, and as I have long finished with youthful vanity – of which I suppose I had my share – I might say that in my eighteenth year I was grown to my full height of six feet and one inch, my build strong but flexible, my countenance well enough, my hair black and my eyes blue.

The landlord's daughter, whom I will not name, as she is still alive and a much-respected grandmother, would bring me coffee and rolls in my room, while I was still in bed. I enjoyed her company and would occasionally give her a shilling for herself, thanking her for her solicitude and kindness. Being still in such matters a complete greenhorn, I did not imagine that the little hussy had other ideas in mind and was therefore astounded when one morning, after depositing the coffee and rolls on the night table, she perched herself on the bed and kissed me soundly.

'What is this?' I asked her, trying to laugh but at the same time blushing hotly.

'You are a nice boy,' she told me, 'but I should think you are not yet a man.'

This remark filled me with unpleasant memories of Miss Armstrong. I pretended to misunderstand her by saying that although I was not a man in years I had had much experience of the world and was doing a man's work.

'But you have not yet known a woman' she said, boldly.

'How do you know, miss?'

At this she seemed somewhat confused and hung her head. Finally she found her tongue. 'A woman can always tell.'

I sat up in bed, put an arm around her and kissed her cheek. 'Even if what you say were true, which it is not, being nonsense, you should not be in a position to be able to tell!'

'Ha!' said she, 'listen to grandfather.'

'So be it,' I pushed her gently from the bed, 'but for my part I intend to remain clear of such affairs until I marry.'

'And a prodigious dull husband you will be,' retorted the

little wretch, pouting and flaunting her person at me. For this she got perhaps more than she bargained, and although I should have repented I did not, for no harm resulted and I was careful not to repeat the experience. Indeed, shortly afterwards I left the inn, after making her a handsome present and with the good wishes of mine host.

She wrote several letters to me and at length I met her, by appointment. She hinted at marriage, but I asked her if she could seriously say I had made her any promise or given her any encouragement to suppose I would make her my wife. She answered honestly, 'No; I acquit you of all blame and if you wish it, from this moment I will endeavour to forget all.' I then kissed her and bade her goodbye for ever.

My next procedure was to rent a larger shop, to which I added a circulating library and news room which gave an additional and steady profit.

I was not a little hampered in my efforts by the constant lapse of my father who seemed quite unable to earn a steady living. It occurred to me that there was one commodity which was, and is, always in demand and with this in mind I consulted my mother who was a good cook and, in particular, made excellent bread.

'It is time that you and I made the family fortunes, mother. Father will never manage on his own.' He was nowhere at hand while I spoke, but in any event I was no longer afraid of him.

My mother looked interested. She had told me on previous occasions that she thought I was too old for my years and had too much responsibility to bear, but she seemed very willing to listen to my plan. 'Well now, Kit my dear, what do you suggest?'

I took my dear mother's hand in mine. 'People must always have bread and while they are buying bread they will buy cakes and pies as well. I propose to set father up in a bakery and if you are willing, because I am afraid it will mean hard work for you, you shall make the bread.

Later on, when the money comes in, you can hire a baker.'

The prospect of hard work, to which the one-time Rose of Fazeley was now well-accustomed, did not daunt her. My mother was then thirty-seven years old, having married in her teens, and my father was forty. She had the health and energy for the project.

My father had no objection to setting up as a baker if capital could be found, and so it was settled. I rented the premises and my father who was in some ways a handy-man, built the oven with his own hands. I then supplied £100 and the business was started. When all was completed, he asked me, 'Now Christopher, what am I to do for flour, and bavins to heat the oven?'

I provided the means for him to buy the bavins and then advanced £10 for two sacks of flour. I also bought them a cow called 'Diamond', which supplied plentiful milk, a quantity of which was sold, and this considerably helped the family. The whole sum advanced for the various purposes amounted to £150, the interest of which I was to receive yearly. This I never had, but I have great pleasure in saying that the bakery was a success and kept the family in comfort until the children were started in life; also it provided comfortably for my parents during the remainder of their lives. My father never repaid the £150 and at his death, many years later, he left the sum of £8,000 to my mother and in trust for my brothers and sister. I was not even mentioned in his will, and although for sentimental reasons this saddened me not a little, by that time I was well acquainted with life and was not unduly surprised.

I will complete this glimpse into the future and then have done with the subject. My dear mother, who survived my father by only one year, said to me: 'You are the most successful one, Kit my dear, and your father did not think you needed anything. It was his way of paying you a compliment.'

For love of her I did not dispute what she said, but

reflected on the sad truth that parents do not necessarily like all their children and that some people find it easier to forgive an injury than a kindness. There is much to be learned about the curious processes of the mind and one day no doubt we shall know more than we do now. In the meantime – and indeed for all time – our Heavenly Father knows and understands us all and His ways must be for our final good.

My mother went to her bureau and handed me a small package. 'Your father left these to me and I choose to give them to you, my dear son.'

Unwrapping the package I found my father's gold watch and chain, the latter adorned with a George II guinea. 'The chain and guinea belonged to his grandfather,' said my mother, 'take care of it, for it will outlive the watch and can pass to your grandchildren.'

CHAPTER 3

During the next few years my business increased and to the selling and printing of books I added publishing, on a small but selective scale. I was anxious to enlarge this side of my activities and knew that having the patience and the will, I would no doubt eventually fulfil my ambition. I was helped wonderfully in my endeavours by the wide popularity of *Waverley*, for which I received large orders. Although the author was at first anonymous, there were few of us in the trade who did not guess his identity.

Having now reached the age of twenty-four years, I began to think of the Propriety of Marriage. I had been cautious in my attitude towards the fair sex, not because of a lack of mutual attraction but due to my fixed determination to marry to my financial advantage. As I also wished to be able to love my future wife, the task I had set myself was not easy.

Somewhat ingenuously I confided my ambition to Mr Charles Taylor, an old friend, who promised me an introduction to a lady of his acquaintance, pleasant but not handsome, and the possessor of a snug little fortune. Mr Taylor added a warning: 'If you do not fall in love with the lady, you had better make sure she is good-natured.' On my enquiring as to how I could do this, Mr Taylor suggested that it would not be beyond my ingenuity to find a way. He then arranged a tea party at his house, to which both I and the lady, Miss Sophia Young, were invited.

Observing her, I wondered why she was not already

married. She was certainly not good-looking in accordance with the standards which prevailed at that time, having a short, kitten-like face, large greenish eyes and luxuriant hair which was so fair in hue that in a bright light it looked almost silver. However, she had a sprightly air and slender figure and I wondered, as her appearance was not entirely unattractive, if she were difficult of temper. If not, I did not think it would be impossible to love her.

As we were the only unmarried pair present, there was a certain amount of joking from the company and I, seized with a mischievous impulse and with my friend's warning in mind, passed a dish of buttered muffins to Miss Young and with a skilful semblance of mischance, dropped the lot in her lap. Seeing the havoc wrought to her silk dress, I was filled with dismay, and fled from the room, taking several turns around the bowling green. When I returned I found the company all laughing and she the pleasantest of the party.

After tea a walk was proposed and I contrived to take her away from the others to a field, where we discovered a tree laden with cherries. Repentant for my trick with the muffins, I asked her if she would like some of the fruit.

'It looks delicious, Mr Wright, but I fear you will have to climb: the cherries have all gone from the lower branches.'

She gave a side glance at my pale blue coat and dove grey trousers (my best) and added sweetly, 'but you will spoil your clothes.'

Not having realised that the fruit had gone from the lower branches and imagining I would only need to reach up and casually pick a few bunches, I secretly regretted my offer, but at the same time was aware that I could hardly withdraw it. I could only hope that as the tree was in a field, far from the smuts of the road, my clothes would not much suffer. The tree was easy to climb and I was poised on a branch, throwing cherries into the held-out silk skirt when there was a loud crack, and the branch which was fortunately not very high, shot me to the ground where I rolled at Miss Young's feet, tipping both her and the cherries to the ground. Burning with embarrassment, I helped her to her feet, badly shaken myself and trying with my handkerchief to wipe from the already damaged dress the havoc wrought by mud and crushed cherries.

'You had better look to yourself,' she said kindly, 'do not mind my dress; it will give me a little occupation tomorrow.'

By this time I was decidedly interested in her and we returned to supper and spent a pleasant evening. At one o'clock I offered to see Miss Young home. There had been a heavy rainstorm during the evening and at the bottom of the garden, by the gate, there was a deep puddle. In my anxiety to help her carefully over it I trod in it myself and splashed her white cloak. She bore this third trial of her temper with such equanimity that I thought: 'Although she is somewhat plain, she possesses very desirable qualifications: good temper and humour and if possible I shall make her my wife.'

A week later I called and took her for a walk in the park, where I proposed marriage to her and was accepted. When the matter was settled and we were walking together, she resting on my arm, she put a question to me.

'Why do you want to marry me, Mr Wright?'

'You will please call me Christopher.'

'Very well then: why do you wish to marry me, Christopher?'

'That is a very strange question!'

'But the answer is very important to me. You see – pray do not speak yet – I have had several proposals of marriage and have refused them because I guessed my suitors were more interested in my money than in me. You cannot have fallen in love with my looks, because I am not considered to be pretty, but you made a trial of my temper—' Here she paused, and as I said nothing, added 'I am glad you do not attempt to deny it, but it will perhaps surprise you to know that I do not mind. You see, Christopher, I knew what you were doing and it diverted me. That is why I let you climb the tree – I thought it would be a small punishment for you, but I punished myself as well; at least, my dress, which really did not matter.'

'I absolutely swear,' I protested, 'that my only deliberate action was with the muffins and I regretted it immediately afterwards. All the rest was quite unintentional.'

'Very well, I believe you and I can see that, like me, you are amused. If we can see humour in the same things I think this will be a very good foundation for marriage—'

As she reached only to my shoulder, I could see nothing of her but the top of her bonnet. Putting a finger under her chin I raised her face, which was alight with laughter. 'Now we are quits,' I said, 'and can be serious,' and taking her in my arms, I kissed her with much enjoyment. Her lips were sweet and warm and I could tell it was not the first time she had received kisses from a man.

I did not love her to distraction, but she filled me with desire and I was impatient for the wedding. I knew, with gratitude and without vanity, that she was in love with me and believed she was right to marry me as she had never loved anyone before.

Mrs Taylor, who was fond of her, noticed she seemed pale and fragile, in spite of her happiness, and asked if she were well in health.

'It's my stupid digestion again. I get such pains – but I think I am nervous and this makes them worse.'

When this was reported to me I did indeed think that she was, like many prospective brides, over-nervous, which state can derange the digestion. 'You must try to be well, my love, in time for our wedding.'

'I *shall* be well,' said Sophia, with energy.

On the wedding morning, Mrs Taylor found Sophia looking very unwell. 'You must have your breakfast in bed and then you will feel better. Caroline' (my sister, the bridesmaid) 'will help you to dress.'

Sophia, who was shivering, wrapped a shawl about her and declined breakfast, asking for a cup of tea. Trying to smile, she said, 'I shall feel better presently.'

She still looked far from well when Caroline arrived, but allowed herself to be dressed in her wedding gown, progressing so slowly that she was a little late at the church, so that I – the bridegroom – the clergyman and the guests became anxious. When she appeared, on Mr Taylor's arm, she looked so charming that her pallor seemed a fitting accompaniment to her ethereal looks – white lace gown, and white bonnet with pale roses fastened inside the brim against her silvery-gold hair. She made her responses in a clear and steady voice and at the wedding breakfast and reception seemed in good spirits, although everyone then noticed her pallor and that she ate scarcely any of the bridal feast. Honeymoons were not then so usual as they are now and we were to start our married life in our new house after staying a few days with the Taylors, who had kindly prepared their best guest room for us.

Aware by this time that my wife was truly in love with me, I felt a deep tenderness towards her on this account and this sentiment, coupled with my desire towards her produced a very close approach to love on my part, so that when we were alone, I took her in my arms, but was disconcerted to see her shrink from me.

'You must not be bashful,' I whispered.

She clung to me, not in passion but as though for help. 'I am not bashful – I love you.' Her words ended on a sob and tears began to pour down her cheeks, 'But I am in such miserable pain.'

All desire fled and was replaced by the deepest solicitude. Lifting her in my arms, I laid her on the bed. 'Rest there, my love; I will get some brandy. Perhaps that will help the pain to pass.' She smiled and laid her hand on mine. 'No, do not leave me.' Her smile disappeared, replaced by the contortion of weeping. She gave a little cry. 'Hold my hands!'

For nearly an hour I suffered with her, through the alternate bouts of pain and sickness, not daring to leave her, until at last the pain passed, when I was able to rouse Mr and Mrs Taylor, asking the latter to sit with my wife while I fetched a physician who, on arrival, found the patient cold and almost senseless. She rallied for a little while and asked for me, her husband, who after kissing her gently, took her hands and knelt beside her. She smiled at me, very faintly, then closed her eyes. Beneath her lids huge tears welled and then ceased, lying on her ashen face like pearls. Her hands grew colder.

The doctor touched my shoulder. 'Come away, my dear sir. It is all over.'

A great blackness came over me: my heart gave a violent lurch and then seemed to stop. It is my firm belief that at that moment commenced that complaint of the heart which, at first slight, has increased with my advancing years. Then, as the blackness cleared away, I saw the still form and felt the icy hands. Yet I could not believe.

'She can't be *dead!*'

The doctor inclined his head and drew the sheet over her face.

I learned that my wife's death was due to acute inflammation of the bowels, incurable and always fatal. I pray that one day a cure may be found for this painful and deadly disease.*

The Taylors had great difficulty in removing me from the bedside and eventually persuaded me to go to the house of another friend, a Mr Carter, where I stayed for three days and three nights. The funeral was attended by almost everyone in the district and my misery was such that I felt I would never recover from my bereavement.

My wife's death provided me with a well-invested income of eight hundred pounds a year. I must record here,

* Acute appendicitis. He did not live to see the cure. Ed.

upon my honour, that I had in my shock and grief forgotten about the money.

Before her marriage Sophia had made a will in my favour, and the lawyer pointed out to me that this arrangement always saved trouble. I had taken a private huff against him because I felt he thought I had married his unfortunate client for her money, and I therefore replied, after a warm tribute to Sophia: 'I suppose I would have inherited her estate in any event.'

'Not so,' said the man of law, 'the money could be willed as the late Mrs Wright pleased. It formed part of a Trust arranged by her late father and was tied up in such a way that she could dispose of it as she wished. It would not, in fact, have been at your disposal if she had lived.'

There was little I could say and no point in saying it.

'It is always useful to know these things' said the lawyer, and stood up, thus dismissing me.

I left his office with mixed feelings. I could not help thinking that Sophia had deceived me a little. Leaving her money to me in the event of her death was surely the natural thing to do: with equal surety she must have anticipated a long life. Then I realised I was doing her less than justice. It was not her fault that the estate was so arranged and I could hardly have expected her to insult both of us by telling me the facts before our marriage. I adjusted my thoughts: I sincerely mourned Sophia and thought of her with tender gratitude; but next time I could afford to marry for love alone. I prayed earnestly that I would be guided aright and was thankful that I had never fallen into the sin of praying directly for money. The ways of the Creator were strange and unfathomable –. At this point I confess I had the grace to blush hotly at the notion that my poor Sophia had been removed in order to provide me with a fortune. I renewed my prayer for guidance and added a petition for humility.

CHAPTER 4

My sister Caroline informed me that I could not live alone. To this I demurred, reminding her that I had managed quite well before.

'Yes, Kit, but you had not then taken a house. Why have a housekeeper who may rob you and possibly drink? It will be much better for your sister to care for you.'

Caroline, although only twenty years old and very pretty was sensible beyond her years. 'You can come if you like,' I told her, 'and I am sure you will do very well, but I would like to see you married and in your own home.'

'I should like to be married, but I am not likely to get any chances at home and I am already getting on.'

'Twenty is still quite young.'

'Yes, but it has a way of becoming twenty-one, twenty-two and twenty-three and one is by then an old maid, Kit. If I come to take care of your house, later on we can entertain when you are out of mourning and there will be people for me to meet.'

'That will be one for me and two for you,' I teased.

She tossed her head. 'Well, and why not?'

At this we both laughed. Caroline and I had always been very good friends and I truly felt it was high time she had a change.

The arrangement proved to be very satisfactory to all parties and when we had settled down I discovered a seemliness and order in my daily life which had hitherto been lacking. The acquisition of the money had temporarily confused my sense of values and when by the aid of Caroline's cheerful proficiency I recovered my emotional balance I felt a new and gentler sorrow for my dead wife, a sorrow mingled with tender affection. I earnestly wished she had lived, but as I could not bring her back I must make the best of my life for after all, in years I was still very young.

The fact that I need never again struggle to make a living was a spur to my ambitions. In future, I vowed, I would select my wares and my authors with care. Also, I would wait for her whom my heart would tell me to love without reserve and if I did not meet such a one, I would not wed again.

One year later I had amassed enough personal capital to buy the house in the square which by a fortunate coincidence was up for sale. Caroline, usually amenable, openly disagreed with me.

'It is too large: we do not want all those rooms.'

'I may possibly marry again one day and eventually it will not be a bit too large.'

'Of course you will marry and I hope you will have children, but even so—'

'I shall buy it and you can have extra servants.'

We moved into the house after it had been redecorated and well equipped and Caroline had to confess that it was pleasant. There was no basement and the domestic offices were on the ground floor. There was also a bathroom and indoor sanitation, all with running water, very clean and fine.

My sister was at this time being courted by a minor poet named Edward Ball and had almost decided she was in love with him as he was both handsome and agreeable. I had published a book of his verse entitled *Selina, or the Wayward Heart*, which consisted of *Selina* itself – a long narrative poem – and a dozen or so of shorter works.

As *Selina* opened with the lines:

> 'Hence loath'd Seduction to some gloomy cell
> Where gelid winter ever loves to dwell—'

I must confess I anticipated interesting revelations and read the poem with avidity, composing in the meanwhile with the other half of my mind a regretful speech to the poet to the effect that works of this sultry nature could not be permitted to bear my imprint. However, it seemed that Edward had used the word seduction in its broader sense and that Selina, daughter of a village curate and the affianced bride of a local farmer, had merely been enticed away from her home by a lordling and then – unsullied – left to shift for herself. This was proved by the lines:

> 'Alban, she sighed, forgive me, oh forgive!
> Short is the time I have, or hope to live,
> Seduced by art I left my native home
> 'Mid scenes of unknown wickedness to roam;
> Too soon the wretch on whom my soul was set
> Has fled, and left me nothing but regret.'

Although I did not personally care for Edward's florid style I knew it was popular and would sell tolerably well. I bought *Selina* outright for twenty pounds and although it was not a best-seller, I proved to myself that the outlay had been well worth while.

With three pounds of the twenty, Edward bought a gold ring set with pearls and turquoises, concealed it in his tail pocket, and calling on me formally, asked if he might pay his addresses to Miss Caroline Wright.

'I have nothing against you, Edward,' I replied, 'but must enquire your circumstances. I must ascertain that Caroline will be able to live in reasonable comfort.'

Edward appeared to be somewhat confused. 'I have a small patrimony,' he said at last, 'an annuity of two hundred pounds a year.'

'That seems well enough, but I thought you had no money at all.'

Edward coloured and hung his head. 'I thought that if you knew, you would not want to pay me for my poems.'

I stared at him, open-mouthed like any country lout. My

first leaning was to indignation, but somehow humour prevailed. 'That would be cheating,' I said, mildly, 'Anyhow, I suppose two of you can live fairly well on £200 a year and no doubt you will make more money with your writing, especially when it has matured a little.'

Although at the time I was twenty-five years old to Edward's twenty-two, it did not seem absurd, certainly not to myself and apparently not to him, that I should be talking like his grandfather, and indeed, I was older than my years and in every way the senior of the boyish-seeming Edward.

'Then I may ask Caroline?'

'Certainly; and, by the way, she would decide the matter herself, but I appreciate your asking me first.'

Caroline accepted her suitor, wore her ring with pride and then began to fret about what would happen to me when she was married. She need not have worried for I was not concerned about it: I knew I would miss my sister but was glad to get her settled. In any event, Providence had the matter in Hand, for on the following day when I was in my bookshop, the door opened a little hesitantly and a young lady stood on the threshold. I went to meet her and closing the door gently behind her addressed her in the softest tones. 'Can I help you, madam?'

The lady, who was clad in deepest mourning (although I did not know, her garments were widow's weeds) lifted her veil and disclosed a countenance so enchanting that I drew a sudden quick breath and held it.

'Oh, please,' she raised her thickly-lashed gentian blue eyes to mine, 'have you Jeremy Taylor's *Holy Living; Holy Dying?*'

I had indeed a copy of that pious work tucked away on a back shelf. I knew precisely where it was, but was determined to make a business of finding it. Having expelled that first breath I found my heart had quickened its beat. 'Please take a seat,' I offered a chair, 'and I will try to find it.'

As I fished about on the wrong shelf (praying that no other customers would enter the shop) I asked myself agitatedly how I could find out about her: if only my foolish hands would cease their trembling! 'I am sorry to keep you waiting, madam, may I offer you this book of illustrations while I continue my search?' As I passed the book to her, she glanced at my hand. 'Is that a mourning ring?' she asked, 'forgive me, but it looks new. Can you too have suffered a bereavement of someone dear to you?'

I must now confess that in all my life I had never been able to give love without reserve, for I needed someone who would be mine alone. Suddenly I knew that in that respect I had been only half alive until the moment when I was asked this question, not curiously, but with a compassionate sweetness. The book was put aside and forgotten, and seating myself opposite to her I pulled off the ring and showed it to her. 'She died on our wedding day,' I said.

Her eyes brimmed with tears. 'What sadness! Poor lady—'

(No pity for me! I was momentarily cast down.)

'—to die so young; not to be your wife; to miss such happiness. You, of course are heartbroken by such a melancholy event.'

'It is true – but you, madam, you too are in mourning. Someone near and dear?'

'My husband,' she sighed.

'Your husband! but you are so young.'

'I am eighteen,' she replied, with perfect dignity, 'and I was married on my sixteenth birthday.'

I pitied the husband: Heaven might know best, but what earthly felicity that young man had lost!

'Your husband was very young too?' I ventured.

'My husband was in his fifty-seventh year.' She gave me a proud glance, defying comment, but I experienced an almost hilarious relief.

'It must be a great grief to you' I said soberly. Each of

us caught the other's eyes and we both smiled resignedly. 'I am recovering,' she replied, 'He was a kind, good man.'

A thousand questions rose in my mind but I dared not ask even one. Then I had an inspiration. 'The book' I said, 'I am afraid I have no copy, but I can get one. May I send it, or bring it to your address?' I held my breath, but she did not seem at all put out by the suggestion. Feeling in her black velvet reticule, she produced a card which I took and glanced at, concealing my feverish eagerness to learn her name. The card bore a black border with the name 'Mrs Diana Holme' engraved upon it, an address written beneath it. 'This is my aunt's address; I am living with her at present. Our house was sold as part of my husband's estate.' She spoke with some deliberation. 'He left very little property.'

So much the better, I thought rapturously. I have enough for two.

She rose. 'Well, sir, I must go. I shall look forward to receiving the book.' I conducted her to the door and to a small carriage awaiting her and stood on the pavement until it had started. Then I returned, slowly, to the shop.

Her name seemed to light a flame in my mind. Diana. She was indeed Diana. Diana, my heart's desire, you must be mine. I thought of holding her in my arms and covering her with kisses. I imagined the beauty of her form and of her glorious hair released from its bonds. I would offer her passion and reverence. If Diana would marry me, this would be perfect happiness and I would have someone of my own to love.

The following day I presented myself at the house and the servant, having asked my name and business, stated that Mrs Holme was out. This required some rapid thinking, for the obvious course would be for me to leave my wares and so lose my chance of a personal encounter. What was the name of her confounded aunt? Ha!

'May I then see your mistress?'

'My mistress is resting, but I will ask her, if you will

wait in here sir.' She showed me into a small ante-room where I racked my brains in an effort to think of a way to discover the aunt's name, for in those days of greater formality no visitor, especially a man, could hope to linger for even five minutes if he were unaware of the householder's name.

The room contained nothing but a small table and a couple of chairs, but it was richly carpeted and the windows were hung with velvet and screened with Nottingham lace. This, I thought, was not the sort of house where the curtains were washed at home: if they had a visiting washerwoman, then I was lost! Standing on the table and then on the window-sill, for I guessed that what I sought would be at the top and not on the bottom hems, I discovered with satisfaction the name 'Cullen,' in embroidery cotton. I was in this position when the door opened and a small grey-haired lady with a merry eye stood on the threshold. She seemed unmoved by the appearance of a stalwart figure balanced on the window-sill and said: 'Mr Wright, I believe: what are you doing up there?'

After a lightning glance at her left hand, I dropped carefully to the floor and said, 'Forgive me, Mrs Cullen, ma'am; a mouse ran up your curtains and knowing that ladies are afraid of mice, I endeavoured to catch it.'

'That was very thoughtful of you; where is it now?'

Her reply and her placid acceptance of the fictitious situation disconcerted me, as I imagined that she would scream and run from the room – not that I wanted her to do so.

'I do not know; it has disappeared.'

'Well, I must tell Sarah to set a trap. You asked for my niece, I believe.'

'Yes, ma'am; I have some books for her.'

'Books? then you can leave them with me. I will give them to her as soon as she returns.'

The fact was, as Mrs Cullen long afterwards told me,

in her own words: 'I did not believe a word you told me, my dear Christopher, for although I liked the look of you, I did not intend to entertain you without knowing anything about you.'

I sensed something of this at the time and being desperate to see Diana, I was inspired to tell the simple truth. 'I am Christopher Wright, the bookseller, madam, and . . .' but I had no need to proceed.

'Oh, *that* Mr Wright; how fortunate! You are just the person to advise me. My late husband was a keen conchologist and I have added to his collection and am now writing a book on the subject . . .'

Oh, Horror! I thought, then as swiftly came consolation. That sort of book took years to write and would probably never be finished. 'I shall be most interested to see it when it is written,' I told her, 'and if it is not too great an intrusion on your time, perhaps you would allow me to see your collection.'

To this she agreed, saying that we would first take tea. Following her, with the books under my arm, I went to a handsome sitting-room where Mrs Cullen poured tea (accompanied by hot currant scones and meringues, which latter I was afraid to eat, much to my regret) and afterwards produced the collection which, although I knew nothing of shells, did seem interesting, especially as they were supplemented by some excellent water-colour sketches. During my examination of these sketches, Diana entered, and to my delighted astonishment Mrs Cullen left us alone together.

'I have brought you the book, Mrs Holme, and have taken the liberty of adding these too, as a gift. I believe all ladies like poetry.' These were Kirke White's poems, elegantly bound in two volumes. She accepted them with delight, and on her asking the price of *Holy Living; Holy Dying* I replied, 'Please take this also as a gift. I found I had a copy after all and it has been on the shelves for a long time. I shall be glad for you to have it.'

'Mr Wright, you cannot do business in this way.' She smiled as she spoke and in taking the books from me, touched my hand, accidentally I presumed, with most pleasurable effect.

I besought her to accept them, whereupon she nodded, smiled, and placed the books on a small table. As she did so, Mrs Cullen returned and glancing most wisely at us both, announced that she had a further collection for my examination but she would leave it to Mrs Holme to show them, as she must attend to household matters, and if Mr Wright cared to stay to supper, he would be very welcome.

When she had gone, I said to Diana, 'Mrs Cullen is very kind; I am glad you are in her care.'

'She has been like a mother to me, but she is not my own kin, only my aunt by marriage. I have no relatives of my own.'

I thought she spoke a little sadly and I felt a deep longing to cherish and protect her. By the end of the evening I was so deeply in love that I decided to employ a bold stratagem and just before I left I pressed into Diana's hand a piece of paper, accompanied by a gentle squeeze. She, with great presence of mind, kept the scrap of paper covered until I had gone and was able to examine it at her leisure and read upon it the words 'I love you.'

The next day I had to go to London, where I wrote to her emphasising my forlorn situation, a widower, about to lose my sister in matrimony, and expressing the hope that she would forgive my boldness but that I truly loved her and hoped she might consider me as her prospective husband. She replied promptly, but a little coldly, and on my return I sought her at her home.

I told her again that I loved her and wished to make her my wife. She answered me with perfect composure: 'I cannot listen to you, Mr Wright, although I am honoured by your proposal.'

'Do you then love someone else?' I asked her, boldly.

She seemed a little affronted by my question and retorted, 'That, sir, is not your affair.'

I asked her pardon and assured her that my question was put only because of the urgency of my suit, and earnestly renewing my request for her pardon, rose in my despair and chagrin, intending to leave.

'Wait a moment' she said, and indicating that I should reseat myself told me that she could not send me away without telling me that although my proposal was not disagreeable to her she could not undertake to remarry without telling a suitor of her history, and as this was one of which she was much ashamed, she preferred to remain a widow and keep the melancholy tale to herself.

I confess that at this point I was beset by the sin of vulgar curiosity, but this was soon displaced by my sincere private and spoken avowal that I could not believe one so beautiful and gentle could have any cause for shame or regret.

'Then if you are willing to listen, I will tell you and you can see how you are minded when I have finished.'

Neither she nor her mother, she told me, had been born in wedlock. Her grandmother, a beautiful French girl, had been chosen among others by Madame Pompadour to grace the court of King Louis XV and provide him with illicit amusement. Diana's mother was the monarch's child and was brought up in pleasure and luxury, eventually becoming the mistress of a French nobleman. Diana was their child, but her parents, not wishing to be encumbered by her, sent her when she was but five years old to England, to an Anglican convent, where she grew up knowing nothing of the tender love of parents and the shelter of a happy home. Diana had no wish to become a nun, and at the age of sixteen was married to Mr Holme, who treated her kindly but for whom she had no sentiment but a mild and grateful affection.

'You asked me,' I said when she had ended her story, told with many hesitations, 'how I would be minded when

I heard your history.' Diana raised her eyes to mine and gave me a look so timid and loving that I could only take her hands in mine and cover them with kisses. 'Your history is nothing to me except to fill me with the desire to love and care for you during my whole life.'

Thus I succeeded in winning the lovely widow, grandchild of King Louis XV and a courtesan, but showing no trace of this mixed heritage in her character, although through two generations she had inherited her grandmother's beauty. How thankful we must be to that great Creator who refines the gold in the furnace and out of evil brings forth good!

Two months later Diana and I were married in the parish church. This time there was a honeymoon and when we were together in the hotel bedroom Diana, who had seated herself on the bed, her bridal skirts of pearl-grey satin spread about her, put her two exquisite hands together and bowed her head over them. I glanced at the clustering auburn curls, as lustrous as her gown, and with a smile asked her. 'Are you saying your prayers?'

She raised her head and there was laughter in her eyes. 'I am trying to find words.'

I seated myself beside her, my arm around her waist. 'For what, my lovely one?'

'I have a confession to make.'

'Then make it – I shall absolve you.'

She leaned her head on my shoulder. 'You were never a husband, and I was never a wife, except in name!' Then, as I took her in my arms, 'I am all yours, Christopher!'

CHAPTER 5

My business was now doing well and I had added to my profits and prestige by a transaction with the Duke of Sussex on whom I had called at Newstead Abbey with some rare books, bought by a lucky chance at a sale by a fellow bookseller who had recently gone out of business. The Duke paid the high price commanded by such books, but added a complaint to the effect that he normally had to pay very high prices for any books he bought.

'May I ask how you conduct your purchases?' I asked.

'My librarian, Mr Pettigrew, attends sales and buys them for me.'

'Might I suggest, sir, that you commission some respectable bookseller to buy for you? Your Royal Highness will realise of course that in the present circumstances the sellers, who know Mr Pettigrew, realise for whom the books are intended and raise the prices accordingly.'

'Just so. Perhaps you would perform this service for me?'

As this had been my intention, I wasted no time in protests but promptly and courteously undertook the commission. This connection proved to be a steady and very lucrative one: the Duke was a book-lover and paid promptly for his purchases with cheques drawn on a London banker which were always honoured, a circumstance which seemed not always to be the case, as I deduced from gossip to which I listened but never contributed. Later, when visiting London, I called at Kensington Palace, at the Duke's invitation, and had the privilege of seeing his fine library of rare books.

I had at that time a stock of about 20,000 books, the most valuable part being works on topography and country history. There was a small but steady demand for these and such was my personal enthusiasm that I began to overstock them. Diana was in the shop one day when I unwrapped a fresh parcel.

'Have you anything interesting there?' she asked, and when the contents were revealed, pouted a little.

'I do not expect you to like them' I said, indulgently.

'I have read all the interesting books in the library and now that I cannot go out much I would like something to amuse me.' She made a small grimace at the books on the table.

I surveyed her with mingled amusement and tenderness. She was eight months with child and carrying her burden cheerfully, but her blue eyes seemed too large for her face.

'You see,' she went on, 'if you buy too many of these books they may depreciate in value. Things do, you know, and I think you should consider the taste of women readers more than you do.'

I thought that madam had made a point, but I was not willing to make the concession. She was a perfect wife and would no doubt be a fond and careful mother, but I considered – in my youthful arrogance – that she knew nothing of business.

'Well, what do you suggest, ma'am?'

'Magazines would be the thing. They are a quick sale and ladies will like them for the pictures and the stories, especially the ones written in instalments. It makes them want to buy the next one, you see.'

'I will think about it.'

When she left the shop I began to ponder. The result of her advice was that I acquired the agency of *The Penny Magazine*, *The Saturday Magazine* and later, *The Pictorial Bible* and *The Penny Encyclopaedia*. This transaction brought in an extra £1,000 a year and (as I thought) I quenched my wife's vanity by saying that for love of her I had consented to sell these trivialities.

Diana smiled. 'But at least they are not trash, dear Chris, or you would not sell them,' which effectively silenced me!

Time has taught me that any man who imagines a woman to be incapable of taking an intelligent interest in business is a conceited dolt. If there is any doubt on this point, let him ask himself who manages the household? The excellent example of my dear mother should have given me better sense, for although I provided the capital it was she who conducted the business and this performed by one who had been bred a fine lady, as unaccustomed to earning her living as my father had been. Doubtless in years to come, women will be allowed more knowledge of their husbands' business affairs and permitted to supply loving and considered counsel without being subjected to disparagement.

Our daughter, Mary Anne, was born at 7 o'clock on a golden September morning. The actual birth was mercifully not difficult, but my wife's frame was slight and after the event the doctor told me I could not see her until later in the morning as she had been much exhausted and had mercifully fallen into a deep sleep. As for the infant, which was hearty enough, it was asleep beside its mother, who would no doubt want to be the first to show it to me.

I looked at the date and then started. By a strange coincidence it was the same as that of Sophia's death. 'The Lord giveth,' I murmured to myself, 'and the Lord taketh away—' Diana would sleep for at least an hour and I must pay my annual visit to Sophia's grave. Leaving the house, with a bunch of late roses plucked from the garden, I took the half hour's walk to the cemetery, where I placed the flowers on the grave, said a silent prayer and returned. When I reached the house, I was met by a servant, who cried 'Oh sir, the missus has been asking for you this long while.'

I went swiftly upstairs to Diana who, supported high on her pillows, held our daughter in her arms. Tenderly I embraced them both and then, at Diana's invitation, taking my firstborn from her, carried the infant to the window, to show her a first glimpse of the world, then amid laughter from us both, took her outside the room and up two stairs, to ensure her progress in life! I would here remark that Mary Anne, being a plump infant, was even in those first hours of her life a very pretty little girl.

I returned to Diana and seated myself beside the bed. 'Where have you been?' she asked me, smiling, 'they could not find you.'

I told her and was alarmed to feel her hand withdrawn sharply from mine and see her pale cheeks flush hotly. 'So you visited her grave and took roses. You could not wait until you had seen me and your child and you did not bring me any flowers.'

Distressed and confused I tried to explain, but only caused her tears to flow. 'It is just a duty, my love, and I thought it should be done.'

'So you say,' she allowed me to dry her eyes 'but you need not have gone today.'

'I must always visit her grave.'

'But not, surely, on your daughter's birthday,' she said coldly.

For a moment I felt helpless, then I recovered. 'Well now,' I said, as lightly as possible, 'what does it matter? As for the flowers, they are all yours and here' – I put two fingers in my fob pocket, 'is something to mark the occasion. Just bend your lovely head.' She did so and then looked down to see, suspended on a fine gold chain, a locket of blue enamel and diamonds. 'Open it,' I said. She pressed the catch and found inside a lock of my hair. 'You see on the other side there is a place for the baby's hair.'

Her tears were replaced by happy smiles, and all was

well. I thought of asking her if I was forgiven, but suppressed the impulse. The less said the better.

The cloud passed and our happiness increased. Our little Mary Anne continued in beauty and closely resembled her mother. When she was five years old, I commissioned a local and gifted artist to paint Diana's portrait. 'You will never be more beautiful than you are now,' I said to her, 'so this is the time.'

'And what about you?' she asked.

'We will wait until I am older and look like the head of a family,' I replied, 'it does not matter about my looking beautiful.'

Diana put her arm through mine. 'You do as you think best; you will get even handsomer as you grow older, I have no doubt. Men have the advantage over us women in this way.'

Such playful remarks as these, and her manner, light-hearted and ever kind, made her loved not only by me, and dearly, but by all who knew her.

Her portrait – for ever young and beautiful – hangs before me now, as I write. Oh, my Diana, how my heart still weeps for you after these long years.

At this time, my traveller having sustained a broken bone in his foot, it became necessary for me to travel the terrain myself. This I was reluctant to do, not wishing to leave my wife with the cares of the business on her hands. However, she reassured me, telling me that she would ask Edward, my brother-in-law, to help with the bookselling during my absence. When I expressed doubt, she said: 'It will do him good to do some real work.'

'He is writing a novel at present and it promises very well: after all, what would we do for a living if authors ceased to write books?'

'You are right, my love,' she agreed, 'I was joking; but it will surely not delay his writing too seriously. You will not be away for long?'

I assured her that my business could be done within a week. 'Then let us ask him and perhaps they can stay here? Caroline can bring Louisa, and she will be fine company for Mary Anne.'

During this conversation between her parents, Mary Anne, who had been plying her needle, put down her sampler and gave a tremendous sigh. Then I could see the little puss steal a glance at her shoes which were new ones, with straps – very modish, as all her friends were, she had assured me, still wearing sandals. Our daughter, at five years of age, was very conscious of her appearance which was most engaging, and promised great beauty in maturity. She was a golden blonde, with a peachlike skin, dimples and a roguish smile which lighted her dark blue eyes – several shades deeper than those of her mother, but with the same thick dark lashes.

'How much have you done today?' asked Diana.

'Just the little tree, Mamma; oh, I am so tired of it. I don't think I was meant to be a needlewoman.'

'Ladies,' I observed, 'do not say "don't".'

'Don't they, Papa?' she inquired. (Now how much of this was innocence? I decided to ignore it; always the best policy when children, or anyone else for that matter, are trying to get the better of you).

'You can put it aside for today' said her mother, smiling, 'there is no hurry to finish it. It will last for many a year after it is done.'

'How long did you take to do yours, Mamma?'

'Not so very long, but then you see I was brought up in a convent, and needlework was very important.'

'I can read it now,' announced Mary Anne, 'I mean read it for myself. I have known it by rote for ages, of course.'

'Yes,' returned Diana, with a glance at me, 'Papa and I are very pleased with your reading and writing and your music—'

'—And when you know your multiplication table better, we shall be even more pleased,' I added.

Mary Anne pouted a little. 'I do try, Mamma and Papa.'

'That is good, my dear,' I said, 'Nothing beats trying except doing.'

Mary Anne looked at her mother's sampler and then spoke the words:

> 'Be thou the first true merit to befriend,
> His praise is lost, who waits till all commend:
> How vain are all our glories, all our pains,
> Unless good sense preserves what beauty gains.'

'I think I understand the words better now, Mamma.' I had turned away, and was busying myself with some accounts, but I heard Mary Anne say: 'Mamma, I am very pleased with my shoes. Should I try not to be too proud of them?'

'I would not call too much attention to them, my dear; especially before Papa, or when you are older, show off before any gentleman, for they like young ladies to be modest.'

Mary Anne seemed to consider this at length. Then she laid down her sampler and leaned her blooming cheek against her mother's shoulder. 'Mamma, you are the most beautiful person I know: are you modest?'

Her mother neither laughed nor reproved her. 'I have learned to be,' she replied, 'now Papa and I wish to talk. You can put away your work and then go up to Nurse.'

Mary Anne thrust the work into her sewing bag and heaved a great sigh of relief. She kissed her Mamma and taking my held-out hand, dropped a small curtsey. I sensed some irony in the action, for I had intended to draw her to me. Here, in spite of her little years was a woman in miniature: anxious for praise; disliking criticism.

I released her hand and frowned slightly. 'Please close the door very quietly when you go, my child; I have a headache.'

Mary Anne, without commiserating with me, tiptoed

out of the room and closed the door with exaggerated softness. I caught my wife's eye. 'There is something pert about our Mary Anne,' I hazarded.

'Oh no, Chris; she is very obedient and thoughtful; she wants to please you. I am sorry you have the headache. Perhaps you are tired. I will ring for tea: a good cup will do you good.'

Later, when we were drinking our tea, she reverted to my comment.

'I do not want you to feel that Mary Anne is pert,' she began, 'on the contrary she is somewhat timid, and needs praise and encouragement. When she seems to be affected by criticism, it is not because she is vain but because she feels discouraged. For instance, she finds it very difficult to learn her tables and is trying very hard.'

'I do not want to be harsh,' I conceded, 'but children must be corrected if they are not to be spoilt.'

'That is true, but what do we know about them, except what we can remember of our own childhood?'

'Surely,' I said, 'it is not difficult to fathom the minds of these little people?'

'I think, as I have said, that it can only be done by trying to remember how we felt when we were children. I remember how much I longed for praise and affection: after all, we expect it from one another, do we not?'

I shook my head and did not answer, not from surliness, but because I was thinking.

At the end of the day I recorded this episode with Mary Anne in detail, while it was still fresh in my mind and with the observation that the dear child's tendency to pertness must be corrected.

I set it down now with the comment that I still had much to learn.

CHAPTER 6

On the Monday, the morning tempestuous beyond anything that might be conceived for the season of late summer, I set forth from Nottingham to Newark where, on arrival, I took luncheon. In the afternoon I attended to my business for two hours and then took a chaise to Grantham where I rested at the Red Lion, the host and hostess extremely civil and the charges moderate. In the morning I called upon my friends and transacted business to my satisfaction.

On Tuesday I proceeded to a village named Cottersworth, where there was the smallest bookshop I have ever seen, kept by a very old gentleman who, I could not avoid thinking, must have found it hard to make a living. He told me he supplied books to the owner of a large estate nearby and by doing regular business was able to make a living, albeit a scanty one. I asked him if it were not a precarious livelihood, to which he answered in a wonderfully meaningful way that this customer felt himself under a moral obligation to the bookseller. Seeing that he was not averse to telling me the reason, I asked 'How can that be, my good sir?'

He then told me that he was related to Sir Isaac Newton and that many years ago he recovered this estate which formerly belonged to Sir Isaac and being in indigent circumstances, sold it at a very low price to the father of the present owner, who hearing the history and how the descendant of the great man was existing in poverty, promised to give regular custom so long as the old gentleman should live. Such are the variations of this transitory life.

I left this village for Stamford, where I arrived at 10 o'clock and put up at the George and Angel, not a first-rate travellers' house but very respectable and the charges fair. For supper, which was cold, the charge was 2s. 6d. I found Stamford a flat town for trade, so continued to Warnsford (in England), still so called from a tradition recorded on a village signpost of a man who during hay-making season at the time when the river was high, fell asleep upon a haycock and, the flood gaining on him, was carried down the stream and drawn under the bridge, where he awoke, and seeing himself surrounded by water and supposing he had been carried out to sea, shouted: 'Where am I? For God's sake where am I?' He was answered by some people on the bridge: 'Warnsford,' at which he cried, 'What! Warnsford in England?'

Three miles from thence is Yaxby Barracks, a depot for French prisoners, containing at that time seven hundred.

My next journey was to Huntingdon, where I crossed the Ouse on a bridge said to be built of stones from some of the churches demolished by Oliver Cromwell. Oh, Cromwell! what devastation thou hadst made in this envied little Island, yet still its pre-eminence is acknowledged by her enemies and always will be while the ships are as well manned as at present by those brave Tars who at all times so nobly defend their native land! This digression is caused by hearing those Jacobins rail against the country by which they are protected and in which they have accumulated (from low origins) sufficient property to retire from business.

After transacting some business in Huntingdon, I took a chaise to Cambridge to the Red Lion Inn. Business was not so good here, and in any event I do not like this town so well as Oxford. However, there is much to admire. I visited the King's Chapel where the windows, carvings and sculpture are very fine: the view from the top of the chapel is extensive, Ely Cathedral to be seen very plainly and the surrounding objects picturesque and pleasing. I viewed the

University Library and the Senate House, in both of which I was much gratified. I was shown an Egyptian mummy, said to be two thousand years old. It was very much decayed by the universal conqueror, Time, but the shape was good, considering its age. How solemn a thing is this Death, which levels all alike and consigns all to oblivion. Let us therefore, while we can, be generous to alleviate the wants or the pains of others, both for virtue's own sake and in the sure hope of a Hereafter.

I was led to these reflections by a conversation I had with a very old man whose granddaughter, sole survivor of his large family, and only sixteen years of age, died of a decline. 'She need not have died, good sir,' he said to me, in trembling tones.

I begged him as kindly as I knew how, to tell me the melancholy history.

He told me she was a good and pretty girl who worked very industriously at washing and mending in ladies' houses, her weekly earnings, which supported her grandfather and herself, being in the neighbourhood of ten shillings. 'She was lighthearted,' said the old man, 'and as kind to me as an angel. Well, with her looks it was natural she should have followers and she chose a young fellow who worked at a mill, up the river.' Here his speech became broken with grief, and of the remainder of this sad tale I can only give the substance.

Both the young people being very poor, and each with family cares, their marriage seemed but a forlorn hope, and nature eventually having its way with them, the girl became with child. To her grandfather only she confided the secret, saying nothing to the young man, whom she ceased to consort with, knowing they could not marry and being unwilling to add to his burdens.

At this point I interrupted, asking if they could not have married and come to live with him, but he told me that the young man's mother was a widow with six children younger than he and that apart from his weekly wage of twenty-one shillings a week, they had nothing but what his mother and the older children could earn by making paper bags at the munificent payment of one halfpenny per hundred.

The girl, when her condition became apparent, was dismissed by her ladies, and being desperate for money, undertook heavy field work, where the employers were not so nice in their judgment. Because of this drudgery she lost her child prematurely and fell into a decline which ended in her death. The old man was then taken to the workhouse.

'She did wrong, I know,' he said, 'but it seems a cruel hard end for her.'

Unable to express adequately my pity and indignation, I could only press his hand within mine and beseech him to honour me by accepting a sum which would help to provide him with some modest comforts. He tried most honestly to resist me, but in the end yielded on my assuring him that it was right for one Christian to help another.

On his telling me that a tombstone had been raised to his granddaughter in the churchyard, I was puzzled to know by whom the money had been subscribed and was informed that it was given by a society for instituting morality among the lower classes. Still incredulous, I sought the churchyard, armed with particulars of the unfortunate girl's name and age, and found the following inscription on a plain granite headstone:

> 'Avengeful death deprived me of my breath
> My soul departed to a World unknown,
> Malignant passions are the sons of hell,
> Christ the deliverer and Christ alone.
> If fiends so vile have dwelling in thy soul,
> Be warned and flee to Christ to make thee whole.'

'Bad verse,' I said aloud in the solitude of the churchyard, 'and cruel sentiments! Dear Lord and Father of us all, thou hast taken this wandering lamb to dwell at peace with Thee. Bless and keep her for all eternity.'

On Thursday, after indifferent business at various small places, I arrived at Lyng, and after a hearty dinner of Norfolk mutton, went in search of a friend of my sister Caroline, who had asked me to see how she did. I took tea with the lady and her husband, whom I found a very agreeable companion but a little touched with Jacobinism. Their politeness and affability were pleasant in the extreme and they gave me a pressing invitation to their house in London, where they were accustomed to spend the winter. The next day, being market day in the town, I had an opportunity to contrast the manner of the Norfolk farmers with those of my own locality and candidly speaking, I preferred the latter. Very few of these Norfolk farmers came to market without carriages of various types, many had two servants in livery and very few indeed were without one. This would have been well enough if they were men of fair dealing, but I was told on good authority that these cormorants held in their own hands five thousand acres of land and of course had the means of withholding grain from the market when they pleased. Thus the poor and labouring classes of society were deprived of earning sufficient for their families by these overgrown monopolists.

That evening I started the journey back to Nottingham. A gentleman offered me a seat in his gig as far as Downham, where I was to pick up the coach. However, after about eight miles his horse unfortunately became lame and in order not to miss my connection I set off to walk the remaining distance. On my way I was benighted and coming to a wood where the roads parted I was at a loss how to proceed, the night being too dark to see the direction on the signpost. I seated myself by the roadside with the intention of waiting until some friendly shout saluted my ear. Presently, hearing the sound of a trotting horse, I stood up to wave and attract the rider's attention, but was not a little dismayed when a coarse yell assaulted my ear, accompanied by an order to stay on the spot if I valued my life and he on the horse would deprive me of my valuables. Tired as I was, this salutation drew from me nothing but exasperation and not believing – although I do not know the reason for my confidence – that he carried a weapon, I called back that if he dismounted we would prove who was the better man. I had no weapon but my bag, containing a few clothes and otherwise laden with books, but a buffet from this could be formidable and I stood with it ready for assault. As we could not easily see each other in the darkness, we sidestepped for a few moments for all the world like the partakers of some absurd gavotte, and then when he was near enough, seeing that he was only about half my size, I gave a leap and knocked him flying. After this, he grovelled about, blubbering for mercy, and tired of this buffoonery, I said, 'Up on your horse and take me behind, for I must get the coach at Downham.' We trotted off at a smart pace and on our arrival when I was able to view my fellow-traveller I discovered a wizened little man who begged me in quavering tones not to hand him over to the law.

'Be off,' I said, controlling my laughter, 'here is your fare. I advise you to leave highway robbery alone; you are not cut out for it.'

During my journey homewards I was filled with an increasing sense of unease, for which I could not account. When I arrived, I found the ground floor of the house, except for the hall, in darkness, but much light in the bedrooms. The servant opening the door before I had plied the knocker, cried 'Oh, master, thank the good Lord you have come for there is such trouble in the house!' and fell to sobbing and crying.

At this moment, my sister Caroline entered the hall carrying a tray and reproved the girl. 'I am sorry you are greeted like this, Kit, 'she said, in her kind and sensible way, 'come and sit down at once, you look quite shocked, and I am not surprised. Lydia, please to carry this tray upstairs when you have taken your master's coat.'

The girl, her sobs reduced to sniffs, went upstairs and Caroline took me into the little back parlour where there was a cheerful fire. 'For God's sake what is the matter?' I asked, 'Is it Diana?'

'Diana is well,' she returned, almost pushing me into a chair and handing me a glass of cordial, 'but Mary Anne has been seized with a high fever and the doctor is not at present sure of the source of the trouble.' I feared for my child and I feared for Diana, who was three months gone in pregnancy.

'I must see them.' I put her aside and got to my feet, but unsteadily, for my heart was making such a clamour that it seemed to shake my whole frame. Caroline restrained me. 'You had better not see the dear child for the time being, Kit. The trouble may be scarlet fever. We are not letting Diana go near her yet, but Lydia and I have had the fever and we are caring for her at the moment.'

'Then what can I do?'

'Go up to Di; she is in your room to be near at hand, although she may not go in.' She laid her hand on my arm. 'Drink the cordial, you look ailing and you do not want to give Di any added concern.'

Strengthened by the cordial and with a prayer for help, I was able to make my way upstairs to our room, where Diana, who was seated quiet and pale by the fire, rose and came to my outstretched arms. Then taking my hand she led me to the fireside where we sat together and spoke of our fears, but softly, each mindful of the other.

'If she has the scarlet fever they will take her to the fever hospital and I am so afraid for her. She has never been away from home – our dear child.'

I tried to find words of comfort. 'If she is in the hospital with the scarlet fever she will not know us anyway and when she is better and knows us we can visit her.' This was frail consolation, but Diana knew I was trying to help us both and she did not argue with me or wail as some wives would have done, but held my hand very tightly and thus we sat together until halfway through the night when the doctor came, for he had told Caroline to summon him if there were a change.

My sister came to our room. 'Kit and Di, please come – the doctor will tell you—' Our hands still locked together, my wife and I went on to the landing. 'The fever has passed,' said the doctor, and when we both smiled at each other with relief, he lifted his hand. 'I am deeply sorry to tell you, my dear Mr and Mrs Wright, that the child has suffered a series of convulsions and she is sinking fast.'

We did not utter a sound, but followed him to our child's bedside where we sat beside her for a full hour. Then for a brief moment she was conscious and looked about to speak. Diana, the child's hand fast in hers, bent over. I could not hear Mary Anne's voice, but I heard Diana's reply which was, 'Yes, indeed, sweetheart.' Then our child fell into a sleep from which she did not awake.

When afterwards we sat together, as yet tearless, for our hearts were too heavy for weeping, Diana suddenly said to me, 'Oh, Chris, do you know what she said? She said "May I have the little cat?" She had wanted one so much and we would not let her have one.'

I searched for words. 'But then you told her she could have it.'

'But it was too late: she wanted it so much and she was so disappointed.'

'I suppose,' I said, 'when we lose someone we love we always have these regrets. We did what we thought was right. I wish I had not corrected her so much.'

Diana sighed deeply and was silent for a long time. Then she said. 'Let us try never to anger or wound each other – '

I understand and I have always remembered. If I have at times sadly failed it is not for the want of trying.

There is truth in the old saying that troubles never come singly. Diana bore herself with wonderful fortitude until after Mary Anne's funeral when she suddenly became alarmingly ill and took to her bed, suffering a miscarriage of her child, with the most fearful accompaniments.

Days afterwards, when she still lay white and spent, the physician spoke privately to me. 'Mrs Wright is recovering slowly and I have every hope she will regain her full health and strength, but I must inform you that for her to have another child would endanger her life.'

Many weeks later, when Diana was herself again, although she never recovered her earlier bloom, I spoke of this matter and its full implications. There had always been perfect confidence between us and although I believe that all those years ago there was much greater reticence between husbands and wives than there is in these days of greater freedom, we had never hidden from each other those deepest thoughts and feelings which concerned us both. (I believe that every human being needs to preserve some secret places in his nature, known only to him and his Maker, but that is a different matter).

'Chris, my dear,' she said, 'this is not to be borne. How can we so live for the rest of our lives?'

'It is your life which we must preserve,' I said.

Here she burst into tears. 'My wretched life! What is it without the comfort of my husband and the joy of my children?'

For once, being sore at heart myself, I could find no words to console her.

The same day I found her, very pale and distracted, making a great blaze in the parlour grate. On my inquiring what she did, she indicated that she was burning the baby clothes.

This sad chapter in our lives makes heavy reading and I will bring it to a rapid end. Diana never recovered from the shock of Mary Anne's death and the loss of the infant on which she had built such prayerful hopes, and three months later she followed our little darling daughter to the grave, where they lie together, in death undivided.

CHAPTER 7

There is nothing significant to record during the five years following the deaths of my wife and child. I lived my life and went about my business, sad and lonely but not embittered, knowing that one day we shall meet again in a better world.

Caroline and Edward urged me to give up my house and live with them, but this kindly offer I declined, my principal reason being that I do not think any relative, however welcome, should intrude on a family. I except of course those aged relatives who can no longer care for themselves and to whom their children owe a duty of love and solicitude.

For nearly the whole of the five years I had an excellent housekeeper who eventually left me to share a home with a widowed sister. My domestic affairs were then somewhat ruffled by the behaviour of the new housekeeper, engaged for me by Caroline, who by obtaining a satisfactory character from this woman's former employers imagined I would be well suited. First I discovered that she drank and then that she stole, but I could not accuse her for fear of defaming her character, as I did not discover her in the act. However, as my brandy and my small change continued to disappear, I decided I must confront her and demand an explanation.

She was a very quiet, respectable-seeming woman, aged thirty-six years and a widow of some years' standing, so it can be imagined that I did not find it easy to approach her on the matter, but it had to be done and I summoned her to me one evening when I returned from my business determined for good or ill to have it out with her.

She denied everything, not angrily but with an air of wounded rectitude which I found highly discomforting. As I could not very well openly accuse her of being a thief and a tippler, I was about – for want of inspiration – to dismiss her to her duties, when she startled me by exclaiming, 'Oh, Mr Wright, sir; oh, my master! I have found this house a haven of peace and kindness since my late lamented husband was taken from me.'

This dramatic form of address, coupled with the reference to her husband who I had understood to be something of a scoundrel, was followed (to my distaste) by her sinking to her knees beside me, seizing my hand and covering it with kisses.

'Now, now,' I protested, 'there is no need for such a demonstration. Just see to my comfort and watch my belongings carefully and no doubt all will be well.'

This seemed to quieten her and she departed submissively, but late that night, when I had retired, there was a scuffle outside my chamber door which burst open to admit madam in her nightgown, with her hair streaming down her back. Crying, 'Take me to your heart and love me!' She cast herself upon the bed, and although I leaped out more speedily than she had leaped in, I could by that moment's proximity sense the strong reek of brandy emanating from her. I tried to move her gently, but she screeched and clutched my pillow to her bosom, so using some force, although not enough to hurt her, I bundled her and the pillow on to the landing, then bolted the door, against which she battered and shouted. I waited in great fear lest her yells should bring neighbours to the house, but after about five minutes they died away and I opened the door with great difficulty as she was lying against it – to my great relief soundly asleep.

I half-carried, half-dragged her to her room where I laid her on the bed and left her. In the morning she had departed taking a bottle of brandy with her. I neither heard of nor saw her again.

Caroline was much dismayed when I told her, but Edward seemed for some unknown reason to be highly amused, for he laughed at great length and then said, 'A rich and personable widower will always be at the mercy of any woman he takes under his roof, my dear Kit. I wish I could have seen you bundling her out with your pillow which she probably thought was you.' My sister bade her husband not to be foolish but to apply his mind to the problem, whereupon Edward, an excellent fellow in spite of tendency to levity, replied with complete gravity: 'The best thing for you to do, Kit, is to re-marry. You are still too young to spend your life in solitude and we would all like you to become a family man again.'

For a moment I was overcome and at a small sign from my sister, Edward went from the room.

'Dear brother,' she said, seating herself beside me with an air of the sweetest kindness, 'You must not mind. Diana loved you dearly and always thought of your welfare. She is happy in heaven and would not want you to continue your mourning. And now I will tell you: when she was very ill she confided to me that if she had to leave you, she hoped one day you would find another wife. She said to me "I know he would not forget me, but I would not want him to be lonely" and I think this is the time for you to consider her wish.'

This counsel from my sister and her husband caused me some profound thought. My chief problem was that I could not imagine any woman in Diana's place and then it gradually came to me that although no-one could take her place, a new wife could occupy a new place and share with me in a new life. This conclusion being reached, I felt much lighter in spirit.

But could I love again? The answer seemed to come to me as though by inspiration that love is boundless in the human soul which is the poorer for limiting its expression.

Thus, calmer and more hopeful than I had known myself for these five arid years, I sought to plan my life anew.

Some two years previously, a Mr Edwards, a friend of mine, had said, 'I have an invitation to dine with an old friend at Brown Hills, near Burslem, tomorrow and I am sure he will be very glad to see you as a friend of mine.' I gladly acceded to the proposal and accompanied him. We spent a very pleasant day. Our host was Mr John Brettell, of the firm of Wood, Brettell & Co., Earthenware Manufacturers, Brown Hills. In walking home from church in the evening, I happened to relate to my host's sister, Miss Mary Brettell, how suddenly I had lost my first wife and how happy I had been with my second partner. I then said, 'I think Miss Brettell I ought not to occupy your arm, for no doubt some gentleman envies me my present situation.' She told me it did not matter what any other gentleman might think, for she should never marry while her brother continued a widower as he then was, considering it her duty to watch over his children.

Remembering this day and some of the remarks she had made, I now thought that the lady would make a good wife, if she were willing and could be detached from her obligations. With this in mind and having to visit London on business, I called on Mr Edwards, intending to ask him if he could give me any information about Miss Brettell, as to whether or not she was married and where she resided.

After we had talked for some time, he said, 'Oh by the way, Mr Wright, you are just the man I want.'

I asked him if he had any orders for me. 'No; it is another commission. You recollect the day we spent at Burslem?'

'Very clearly,' I said.

'Well, sir, it is now a year since I lost my wife: I am thinking of making an offer to Miss Brettell and I would like you to call on my behalf.'

'She will certainly make an excellent wife to someone,' I said, 'do you know where she lives?' He told me it was somewhere in the neighbourhood of Birmingham and that she kept a boarding school.

I then told him of my own inclination and he said 'I admire your choice and may the best man win, provided of course that the lady is not married. I do know that Mr Brettell has married again.'

'I will be honest with you, Mr Edwards,' I assured him, 'I will speak for you, but I must try my luck too, if she is not willing to accept you.'

To this he answered, 'Do so: I appreciate your sincerity. Tell her that upon my honour, if she will have me I would marry her tomorrow.'

I then went to Birmingham and put up at the Albion in High Street. I very anxiously and frequently studied the newspapers to see if I could find the name of Brettell among the educational advertisements, but was unsuccessful. However, the newspaper office from which I enquired, told me that there were many of that name living at Stourbridge and Kidderminster.

Accordingly off I started the second day to walk to Stourbridge, a distance of two miles from Birmingham. I stopped at a roadside inn for a glass of ale, and asking the landlady if she knew of a lady of the name of Brettell who kept a boarding school in the neighbourhood, she replied no, but that most likely her daughter would, as she had very recently become a teacher and would probably know about the other schools in the vicinity. She then called her daughter who replied, 'Oh, yes mother, I know her very well: she lives at Erdington and is in partnership with Mrs Dunn.'

This explained why I did not find the name of Brettell among the advertisements, as I had merely looked among the B's, whereas it actually appeared thus: 'Mesdames Dunn and Brettell.' I at once altered my route and crossed the country through Aston to Erdington, eventually reaching the house. I rapped at the door and it was opened by Miss Brettell herself. Not expecting to see her so suddenly, I must confess I was very much confused and for several moments could not utter a word, looking extremely awkward and foolish (as she afterwards told me). She held the door open for some time and at length I found courage to say: 'Do you recollect your brother's old friend, Mr Edwards?'

'Certainly,' she replied, 'do you know him?'

I said yes, I had brought a message from him, and upon her asking if I had a letter, I said no, it was a verbal message. She then asked me in, desired me to sit down and to excuse her for a short time as the dinner was ready and the pupils were then sitting down to the meal. During her absence I began to think seriously whether or not (if Mr Edwards's suit failed) I should say anything myself as somehow she did not now take my fancy, being good-looking but somewhat governess-like and missish in her manner.

In about half-an-hour she returned, and offering an apology for her absence, asked me if I would take a little dinner (wishing as she told me later, that I would refuse as there was nothing left). I gladly accepted her invitation, so she had to send out to get a beefsteak. As I was partaking of it, I said that Mr Edwards was very anxious to know if she were disengaged.

She was sitting opposite to me as I ate and between gentlemanlike mouthfuls I tried – modestly, as I hoped, although as she later told me it was the funniest thing to see me measuring her up with my mouth full – to gain a full impression of her appearance. This I found decidedly pleasing.

'That is a very curious question,' she replied, 'but as Mr Edwards is a very old friend of my brother I have no objection to his knowing the answer which is yes, perfectly so. Have you any idea of his reason for asking?'

I had finished the steak and she pushed a dish of fruit

towards me. 'I am sorry there is no pudding; the girls have eaten it all: anyhow, fruit is better for you.'

I thanked her, and peeling a pear said: 'I can soon tell you his reason. He lost his wife last year and wonders if he has any chance of success with you. If so, he will very soon wait upon you.'

'Mind your cravat!' she advised, 'pear juice never comes out. Well, Mr Wright' and here she smiled for the first time, showing dazzling teeth, 'however much I respect Mr Edwards he is too old for me and has too large a family.' (He had four children.)

I had dispatched the pear, much to my relief, and wiping my fingers on the napkin, said 'Well, Miss Brettell, that seems to dispose of that. And now,' I folded my arms and gave her a glance that I hoped was both humble and winning, 'would you consider Mr Edwards's friend?'

Miss Brettell rose, unhurriedly, and with a rather restrained smile said, 'You must excuse me for a minute, Mr Wright, I have business to attend to and will return shortly.'

As she subsequently informed me, she went to Mrs Dunn and said, 'I wish you would go and get rid of that man, I believe he is quite mad and has been saying the wildest things imaginable.' Mrs Dunn accordingly entered the room and said, 'Mr Wright, I have come to tell you that we must not take up any more of your time, as your errand is fruitless.'

She then by chance glanced at the debris from the pear and began to laugh. 'Wait a minute,' she said, seeming not to dislike me. She returned to Miss Brettell and said to her: 'I do not think he is mad, my love; go back and hear all he has to say.'

Miss Brettell returned, and by this time I had made up my mind to proceed with my suit, but was at a loss to know how to re-open the subject, suddenly realising that I was to all intents and purposes, a stranger. It did not occur to me – such is human vanity, and male conceit in particular – that the lady would have no recollection of our earlier meeting. Apart from this, of which I was in any event unaware, Miss Brettell seemed to be a lady of excellent composure and well contented with her lot and (in this at least, I was humble) I wondered if she would consider the proposed change in her circumstances to be to her advantage. However, having proceeded thus far, I must find out.

'Well, Mr Wright,' said Miss Brettell, smiling, 'what is it?'

'Perhaps I should visit you again,' I returned, still somewhat at a loss, 'to tell you what is in my mind.'

She became almost alarmed and looked anxiously towards the door. 'I do not understand; what is it you wish to say?'

'Would you have the kindness,' I asked her, sensing much to my annoyance that I was blushing like a schoolboy, 'to grant me a favour?'

Again she said, 'What is it?'

'I have something rather particular to say, if you will consent to take a walk with me.'

This at first she refused to do, but by this time greatly attracted by her, I persisted, and she consented on condition that Mrs Dunn should bring up the rear. I was at first somewhat hampered by the consciousness of the lady's presence, but my increasing ardour dispelled this embarrassment and I managed to express the hope that Miss Brettell would consider me as her suitor.

'How extraordinary!' she replied, 'I thought you were here on behalf of Mr. Edwards, and although it is true I indicated my disinclination in that direction, I would not have thought you would wish to take his place.'

'Why not?'

'It is not usual for a complete stranger to act so.'

'Miss Brettell: is it possible that you do not remember me?'

'No – should I?'

I recalled to her our last meeting, whereupon to my vexation she began to laugh, although kindly. We were at the time walking along a narrow flagged path which made single file necessary and I was very conscious of the elegance of her carriage and the brightness of her high-curled, hazel-brown hair, above the slender neck. Suddenly she turned and confronted me, compelling me to step back a pace or two. 'I had forgotten' she confessed 'and I hope you will forgive me. On that day I met so many of my brother's friends and as you will realise Mr Wright, I reach only to your chin, so I did not have much opportunity to look into your face.' She gave me the full sunshine of her lovely smile and offered me her hand which I took and kissed, somewhat to her confusion for she had expected me merely to press it.

'Then now I have established my identity may I venture to hope?'

'I cannot possibly express an opinion on the matter now, Mr Wright – our acquaintance is still far too slight.'

'Then may I have the opportunity to see you again?' I was by now much disheartened and as she had reduced me to a proper state of humility and was determined that I should woo her in a proper fashion, she gave me permission to call again in a week's time.

A week later, I called on Caroline and Edward, for their approval before I set forth. On their advice, I was wearing a new suit, as they had told me it was time I discarded semi-mourning. 'That pale buff and dark brown suit you very well' said Edward, scanning my coat and trousers.

'I am glad you have put on the flowered silk waistcoat' added Caroline, 'now Ned, the topaz pin.' She stuck the pin in my cravat while Edward winked at me the while and stood back to admire the effect. 'If that doesn't fetch her,' he said, 'nothing will. Oh – and one other thing, Kit – remove those two mourning rings: they have served their purpose.'

In spite of their good offices and kindly encouragement,

I felt anything but hopeful, but remembering that faint heart never won fair lady, I armed myself with a large nosegay and a drum of French confectionery and presented myself at the lady's house.

It so happened that once again Miss Brettell opened the door. 'Come in, Mr Wright,' she invited me, gravely, and feeling very low in my hopes and awkward in my person, clutching my hat, the posy and the parcel of sweets, I stepped inside, facing her with what I knew was an abashed air. Beckoning me into the sitting-room and closing the door, she said, 'Well, sir?' I glanced at her, happily surprised, for her tone was gentle and she was smiling at me. Although years ago I had foresworn gambling, I took at that moment the greatest hazard of my life, for dropping my hat, the flowers and the sweets on the floor, I took her in my arms and kissed her.

Thus I became engaged to my dear Mary – destined to become my true, loving wife and the mother of my children.

After a charmed hour had passed, Mary suddenly assumed a solemn aspect and said, 'I suppose we shall have to tell Mr Edwards.'

'I must do so: I cannot fail to feel sorry for him.'

Mary looked thoughtful and then, her face suddenly alight with a mixture of mischief and kindliness, she said: 'Shall we introduce him to Mrs Dunn?'

This we eventually did, with the happiest results, for Mr Edwards and the lady were of similar ages, and being for so many years accustomed to the care of other people's children, she found it no hardship to become stepmother to the Edwards family. This, I am glad to say, was a most harmonious marriage.

CHAPTER 8

On the morning of August 7th, 1827, I rose soon after 6 o'clock and commended to the care of our Heavenly Father my dear wife, who was in labour with our first child.

The weather had been hot and sultry and at 6.30 a violent thunderstorm broke. Anxious for Mary, and fearing she would be frightened by the clamour, I knocked at the door and was confronted by the midwife who told me that my wife did not wish me to enter at present and that she was not in the least afraid. After an hour or so, the storm passed over, the sun broke through a rapidly-clearing sky, the birds, interrupted in their dawn chorus, singing most joyfully.

As I stood by the window, feeling suddenly at peace, the door opened to admit the midwife, smiling broadly. 'You have a fine son, sir,' she said, 'and you can see him and Mrs Wright for a few minutes.'

Later, when I was allowed to see Mary for a longer period and had duly admired my son – although to tell the truth he was somewhat small and ugly at this early stage – I asked her: 'What shall we call him – if he lives?'

'What else but Christopher Norton?' she smiled, 'and he is certainly going to live – to a ripe old age!'*

In reply to my question as to whether the storm had frightened her she answered, 'On the contrary, it suited my mood. In spite of myself I cried out once or twice, but you did not hear me, did you?'

* He died in 1912. Ed.

I confessed I had not. 'And when the storm was over, this young man made his appearance. So all is well, my two Christophers.'

Mary never shortened my name. This habit of hers I liked well enough and I never knew whether she used my full name from choice or whether she did so because she asked Caroline how I had been addressed by Diana. We called our son Norton.

When he was nine months old I had to go to France on business. I told Mary that I did not like to leave her, but she was not disturbed, telling me that she was well satisfied with our servants' loyalty and that Caroline and Edward were near at hand. She told me to enjoy the journey and to guard my health. 'Do not carry any heavy bags,' she said, 'find a porter: your heart needs care.'

'How do you know?' I asked her, for I had not complained.

'I know everything,' she returned, 'so mind what I say, my dear.'

Edward offered me frivolous advice. 'Be sure those Frenchies do not swindle you; and watch out for pretty French girls. Indeed, I think I had better come with you to guard you against all pitfalls.'

'You are not going to Paris without me, Ned,' said my sister, 'and there is no need to warn Kit against anyone: he will be quite able to deal with sharks or hussies.'

'I did not say he would not, my love; I merely warned him.'

'And now, after all that nonsense,' went on Caroline, 'we will tell him our news.'

This proved to be the foretelling of a happy event. Louisa was by that time a well-grown girl of ten years, and her parents had given up hope of another child. When I told my wife, she expressed her pleasure and then her hope that Miss Louisa's nose would not be put out of joint as she was, although a dear child, somewhat spoilt and wilful.

'I think not,' I said, 'for Edward has already told her and she looks forward to the event with much interest.'

'Edward has told her! I find this a little shocking.'

I said nothing, for I was thinking.

'. . . But then,' my wife continued, 'he is a poet and a novelist and more free in his manner of thinking.'

'Well,' I said, after some consideration, 'I confess I was a little shocked, too, but now I agree with him and Caroline: we tell children of death – why not of birth?'

My wife shook her head, not entirely convinced, but not displeased.

I was still pondering, for I had not until that moment formulated my views on the matter. 'Our Lord is with us at both events,' I said, 'and each is emergence from darkness into light. That is the way He has chosen for us and there can be nothing shameful about one or the other.'

'What if the children are born in shame?' asked my wife, but not censoriously.

'That is a different point, but as you have mentioned it, I would say that no child is born in shame: it is not responsible for the deeds of its parents.'

'Do you not then believe in original sin?'

'That again is a different point, but my answer is no: nor do I believe an innocent child goes to Hell if it is unbaptised.'

'But it would have been unthinkable to have omitted baptism for our child?'

'Of course, my love.'

My wife smiled. 'I understand exactly what you mean, Christopher.' She turned her attention to Norton, who during his nurse's afternoon out was giving us the benefit of his society. 'Just look what he has done, and he knows how to ask! And you say you do not believe in original sin!'

'That is not very original,' I remarked.

A week later I and my assistant, Mr Clifford, made the

crossing to Boulogne, in favourable conditions and with no untoward incidents, the weather being still and sunny. We stayed in Boulogne for two days, before proceeding to Paris, and on the first morning as the clock struck five, we rose from our beds and at 5.30 sallied out. The tide was very low and a great number of men waited near the shore with one-horse carts, tackle and ropes; also wheelbarrows. The women, coming in from shrimping, carried their nets and bags of shrimps and our English modesty caused us to blush a little at their costumes – no stockings and their petticoats hoisted to the tops of their thighs. However, later in the morning we saw these same females properly attired and selling their shrimps, also oysters, on well-scoured tables. We had some oysters with our dinner which also consisted of a very tasty herb omelette and a cheese savoury, followed by excellent coffee and cognac. I enjoyed this dinner better than our breakfast of two mutton cutlets, somewhat tough and with all the fat removed.

We did some very satisfactory business in this town and the next day continued our journey to Paris. This was uneventful and slow in progress, the coach and the cattle being much inferior to our English equipages. However, the journey was enlivened by the presence and anecdotes of a vivacious French gentleman and his wife, a sprightly and handsome lady in a wondrous bonnet surmounted by ostrich feathers, of which I afterwards made a sketch for my wife's benefit, she having commissioned me to take a note of the French fashions. I could see that Mr Clifford was not a little taken with the lady, but as he did not speak or understand French he was unable to join in the conversation or understand the jokes, although he dissembled very well by participating in the laughter which followed them.

We parted on the pleasantest terms and with arrangements to meet on the following evening, when our acquaintances promised to take us to Parisian haunts seldom seen by the visitor from Albion. This prospect seemed most delightful and we were not a little excited by it, although we accepted the invitation with commendable calm!

We put up at the Hotel de Boulogne, Rue Notre Dame. Here we found the service and the food good, but the beds and sanitary facilities unsatisfactory. Owing to the seasonal influx of visitors to the City, we were obliged to share a room and at first it seemed we would have to share a bed. At this we protested, whereupon the chambermaid summoned the manager, who with many flowery expressions of regret, accompanied by the usual gesticulations, replied that he could offer in addition to the main bed, only the trundle bed beneath it. This was pulled out and after assurances that it would be well aired, we agreed to make do with it.

We dined well on a roast fowl with vegetables, followed by strawberry creams, Camembert cheese and coffee, and retired early, tossing a coin to decide the allotment of beds. Mr Clifford won the toss, but it was agreed that we should sleep alternate nights in the large bed.

About a pint of hot water was produced for our washing and we decided to make up for it in the morning. As there was no water laid on this top floor, the privy, when after much wandering we found it, was of the most dismal and primitive sort. We then understood the reason for the presence in our room of the immense commode which to our astonishment proved to be of twofold accommodation. Cheering each other with the observation that we were staying there for only a few days, we took these drawbacks philosophically; some, indeed, we found amusing.

Lying in my trundle bed which was hard but not intolerable, I was unable to sleep for the noise issuing from the large bed which, as Mr Clifford tossed and turned, resembled the efforts of an inexperienced harpist.

'Can you not sleep?' I asked him, at length.

He shot up in bed and exclaimed, 'This bed is frightful! It is stuffed with rocks and all the springs are broken I think.'

I rose and lighted the candle and together we examined the bed. With the rope from our trunk we managed to tie the springs together and then spent some minutes in pummelling the lumps in the mattress. After this, Mr Clifford cautiously got into the bed and expressed his relief. The next day we begged the chambermaid to find another mattress if possible. She produced a feather overlay upon which that night I lay and stifled. However, these were small matters. We spent the day in sightseeing and returned to our hotel in the evening, footsore but pleased with our excursions, to enjoy another excellent dinner of veal escallopes, followed by a rum omelette.

The next morning I sought Mr Twentyman, the English bookseller in the Jardin des Plantes and did some very satisfactory business, including an advance sale of Edward's new novel, *Bertha* and a repeat of *Calantha*, which had received excellent reviews in the London press. I tried to interest Mr Twentyman in Edward's collected verses, but was told that verse was not in demand at the time. This I had proved to my own dissatisfaction, there being a vogue in these matters, although whether the demand is limited by the supply it is not easy to tell. If I had foreseen the wealth of great poetry which was to issue forth in the reign of our noble Queen I would have been much happier, for it is my considered opinion that when a nation lacks fine poets its culture is in the doldrums.

After spending the day in more sightseeing, we met by appointment at their hotel our two friends, Monsieur and Madame Gagnès. Here we were introduced to an English lady on a journey to Italy as the travelling companion of the Marchioness of Stafford. She was young and very attractive and immediately engaged Mr Clifford's attention. The room where we took tea was lined with splendid mirrors and it was amusing to watch him studying her reflection from all angles while he bashfully averted his eyes from the fair original. After tea, as there was some time to spare before our evening engagement, Mr

Clifford took the lady for a walk and returned (looking both enraptured and foolish) with the promise that he might write to her when he returned to England. This encounter resulted, a year later, in their engagement and marriage.

As the ladies were not to accompany us on our evening excursion, we parted from them with expressions of courtesy and appreciation of their company.

M. Gagnès took us in his private carriage to a building where we descended marble steps decorated on the balustrades with urns of exotic flowers into an underground restaurant, the floor of which was filled to capacity with small tables, attended by dozens of waiters threading their way through the narrow spaces with the speed and dexterity of acrobats. At one end of the restaurant which was brightly lit by handsome chandeliers, was a platform, screened by heavy silk curtains. A small company of musicians was playing on a dais at the side of the restaurant: all was light, cheerful and respectably conducted.

About half-an-hour after our arrival, when we had eaten an excellent meal and were enjoying our brandy, an announcement was made by a portly gentleman wearing a ribbon in his coat that the entertainment was about to commence. The curtains parted on a rural scene which proved to be a tableau representing the bestowal of the golden apple by the shepherd Paris.

The chief feature of this and other tableaux which followed was the scanty drapery of the females concerned in the display. It was all greeted with much enthusiasm from the spectators and under cover of the applause for the first item, Mr Clifford asked me if I did not think it strange that Pallas Athene, who like the other two goddesses, was naked to the waist, should be wearing such a massive helmet. 'It is like putting on one's hat, to take a bath,' he added.

I could say little but that it all seemed somewhat monotonous and that as we had already, during our sightseeing, seen innumerable statues and pictures of females entirely unclad, I could not find anything peculiarly interesting in the present display.

'But these are real women,' Mr Clifford said, 'I find that makes all the difference.'

'They are not permitted to move, though, 'I pointed out.

When the curtain fell, Mr Gagnès asked us if we had enjoyed the tableaux, to which we replied with perfect honesty that it was most interesting and unusual. 'You were not affronted then?' he asked us, smiling, and we assured him we were not. He then asked us to accompany him to an inner room and wondering, with some apprehension, what this implied and with the firm resolve that we would not be parties to any loose behaviour, we followed him, to discover when we were inside the doors that it was a gaming room, in the activities of which we were cordially invited to join.

'You,' I said to Mr Clifford, 'must do as you please, but I long ago made a vow that I would never partake in any form of gambling whatsoever and I intend, hoping that I do not give offence, to keep my vow.'

The expression of M. Gagnès changed considerably when I made this announcement, especially as Mr Clifford obviously intended to support me, and seeing that we were adamant, M. Gagnès ushered us out with a very lowering countenance, informing us brusquely that on the following morning we would receive the account for our evening's entertainment.

This account, which was for one thousand francs, representing nearly fifty pounds, was something of a shock to us and we decided to confide the circumstances to our hotel manager who said it was an essayage, or try-on, and advised us to ask for a detailed account and then refer the matter to our London solicitors. This we did, and heard no more of the incident, which caused me some pangs of conscience for at least we owed them for our dinner. However, they doubtless had some apprehensions in the matter, for we realised afterwards that M. Gagnès had introduced us to this establishment with the express purpose of making us join in the gaming. We had indeed behaved like country cousins, but my willingness to accept his acquaintance may be explained by the fact that as I had travelled so much in my own country, I was accustomed to making casual acquaintances without any thought of double dealing, although, should this prove to be likely, in my own environment I could readily recognise it.

Thus no harm ensued from the incident which, apart from its conclusion, had been diverting.

On the last morning of our visit, which was fine and sunny, we visited the splendid cathedral of Notre Dame and afterwards called at a café where we sat outside at a small table and ordered a bottle of their excellent light wine. The wine was brought to us by a young girl, attractively dressed in a dark silk gown with white ruffled collar and apron. She had very white and dainty hands, and it was these hands, setting out the bottle and glasses which induced me to look up at her face, to see if it matched the hands in refinement, which it did, being delicately pale, with large grey eyes. Her hair was that splendid shade of dark red which has always attracted me.

Knowing by then some of the customs of these places, I asked her if she would be so amiable as to take a glass of wine with us. She said she would ask permission and after disappearing for a minute or so, reappeared without her apron and seated herself at the table. Our conversation, in which as usual poor Mr Clifford was unable to join, was polite and conventional and after I had told her that I was an English bookseller visiting Paris on business, I ventured to ask if it was her custom to work in the café.

She shook her head. 'No, Monsieur; the café belongs to my parents; I am taking my holiday at present and I help them a little. As for me—' and here I must quote her words in French, 'Moi, je suis modiste.'

Mr Clifford, who had been listening with his usual air of vague politeness and by now understood a few simple words such as 'moi' and 'je suis,' looked startled, coloured a little and asked me '*What* did she say?'

'Mademoiselle dit qu'elle est modiste.'

'Oui,' she repeated, smiling, 'je suis modiste.'

Mr Clifford then relapsed into silence and as the wine was finished and it was time for us to leave, I paid the bill with thanks and compliments to our fair hostess and we departed. When we had left the café, Mr Clifford said, 'These French girls seem to be all the same: why did she keep on saying she was modest? Did she think we wanted to take advantage of her?'

After enlightening him, I added the advice that before his next visit to France he should acquire a working knowledge of the language.

Upon my return home, I found myself much engaged with domestic affairs.

Mary, who welcomed me fondly – a dear, good wife in whom I was much blessed – informed me that all had gone well in my absence. She was much entertained by my account of our experiences (although I omitted to mention the half-clad women) and when I produced the sketch of Madame's bonnet, expressed her delight, at the same time saying that she would not dare to appear in anything so smart, apart from the fact that she did not have the ostrich feathers. I thought I perceived some wistfulness in her tone and had the pleasure of producing replicas of the feathers, which I had brought with me as a present from Paris. These, although a little smaller than the originals, seemed to please her greatly and she appeared in church on the following Sunday in her modish bonnet, much to my satisfaction, for I took pride in her appearance.

She mentioned that our gardener, Jem Witham, was due to arrive on the Monday and after a day at the shop I returned for my tea to find that he had cleared out five beds of plants, many of which were well-established favourites. I was sadly disappointed in his day's work and remonstrated with him, whereupon he picked up his tools and said I could do the rest myself. I accused him of ingratitude and reminded him how I had procured a bed for him at the hospital at one hour's notice when he was sick and had paid him during his sojourn there, adding that he could have his wages then and be paid off, or return the next day and do the work honestly and well. He took his wages and went. How sad that much of the old respect between master and man has vanished: the new ways are surely not the best.

On that same day a customer had shown me a newspaper published at Norwich in September, 1728. Since that time how changed is our existence! Vice is practised in various shapes which then were not even named and destructive war has raged with violence; indeed, in my early youth it seemed that we should never be at peace, which at that time had not visited this Island for twenty years, except for a short respite in 1802. When will the great Dispenser of the affairs of men put an end to this senseless despoiler of millions of our fellow creatures? Now we are at peace, but who knows how long this blessing may last and what dreadful form it may take in the future?

Shortly afterwards, we were happy to welcome my youngest brother, James Spurrier Wright, whose visit coincided with that of a Miss Eliza Paget, one of Mary's former pupils. We made a very happy household and by the time of James's departure he had become an accepted suitor for the young lady's hand. Her parents gave their consent with the proviso that James should be settled in some reliable occupation before the marriage took place, as both he and Miss Eliza were very young. This was easily accomplished. I lent him £200 to commence business as a printer and he succeeded so well that his former master, to whom he was apprenticed, was much put about by the competition. He and Miss Paget were married shortly after he started his business and their marriage has been a long and happy one, blessed with four children. James not only repaid my loan with interest, upon which he insisted although I asked for none, but also supplied much useful co-operation.

While the young couple were staying at our house, Mary and I on one occasion entered the room where they were together, to find them laughing heartily over a letter. On our asking if we might be permitted to share in the joke, Eliza replied that the letter was from her grandfather and penned to her when he knew she was preparing to make a round of visits to her friends. This letter, of which my wife begged a copy, is reproduced below.

My dear Eliza,

Your Mamma tells me that you propose to make a round of social visits among your friends, and your grandmother joins me in offering hearty wishes for your pleasure. I offer, too, with the fondest love, my advice to one who is new to the ways of the world.

You cannot but know that a young lady is exposed to a variety of temptations peculiar to her age and sex, especially in the company of gentlemen whose professions and conditions of life may not incline them to the greatest decency and sobriety of behaviour, and it will require great prudence on your part to manage them. Your principal difficulty will be in keeping yourself free from those importunities which are on many accounts inconvenient and must be rejected with the greatest resolution. And here, my child, I would advise you by no means to put on an air of resentment and prudery as though you apprehended some animal design in all that they said and did. There is a kind of reserve, mingled with the most cheerful freedom which restrains the licentious beholder and inspires a reverence for the gentle charmer. This should make a man blush at the secret consciousness of an irregular wish with regard to so excellent and sacred a creature.

After reading this effusion, I remarked with mock gravity: 'The advice is no doubt excellent, but I think you scarcely need it.'

We discovered, although not for some time afterwards, that her grandfather had been something of a rake in his young days, which accounted for his apprehensions!

CHAPTER 9

The New Year of 1831 was a happy occasion for the whole of our family. I was greatly blessed by the kindness and love of my dear Mary and we were by then the proud parents of four children: Norton, Walter, Henry and little Eliza, named after James's wife. It was joyful, after the advent of our three fine boys, to welcome a daughter, but we employed no favouritism among our children: we were well content with them all and let them bring each other up, as the saying goes.

My three other brothers, Henry, William and Walter, were in steady professions, two of them married and one destined to remain a bachelor. James and Eliza, with their children, had settled near us and a year previously Edward and Caroline had departed to London, Edward having achieved success as a dramatist, with two plays running concurrently at London theatres. At Christmas, 1830, I had received the following letter from him:

A very merry Christmas to all you dear people from myself, Caroline and our two lovely daughters, hoping you are all in the best of health and spirits.

I am anxious to consult you about my new novel *Elestra*, which will be finished by Easter, in three volumes. As it was my wish to get rid of Newman in a handsome manner, I offered the work at a price which it would not have answered his purpose to give and of course he pleaded the bad sale of *The Black Robber* as an excuse for declining my offer. The fact is I must be published under a more respectable bookseller than Newman or under none at all. It is true that *The Black Robber* is not so successful as my previous books, but this is hardly surprising because as you know, it was disreputably produced and under-advertised.

I wish I could get into treaty with Longman, but I do not know how to go about it. At all events, I would rather burn *Elestra* than have it published in the manner of *The Black Robber*.

My next play I full expect will be performed by Easter. Richards writes me that Cadell's people are willing to print it and go halves. I do not understand whether by this they mean I should pay for the printing in part, or whether they would set that expense against the MS and allow me an equal share of the sale, deducting advertisements. I can now afford some small hazards, but I would greatly value your opinion beforehand.

Our daughters are blooming. Louisa often speaks of you and her aunt and tells Kitty about you. I wish you could both peep in these cold and frosty mornings and see how cunningly Kitty contrives to steal crumbs from the bread basket and convey them to the birds in the garden, while her eyes sparkle with delight, her cheeks glow with rosy health and her golden curls float in the chilling blast of winter. On awaking this morning she enquired of her grandmamma from whence the light came, for it was always dark when she went to bed. The reply of course was 'From God.'

'And where is God? I have never seen Him.'

'God is in heaven; he does not appear to little girls: God makes the corn grow; He gives good to all things.'

'But not to the little birds,' archly replied Kitty, 'for *I feed them.*'

She begins to read, though reluctantly, but she can say the Lord's prayer in French, with the most beautiful articulation.

You remember our good Dr Nichols? He called on us yesterday saying that he is receiving many of his fees in goods instead of cash. Saunders, the butcher, sent him a piece of pork from one of his own pigs, but the doctor was told in an anonymous letter that the pig fell sick and Saunders was forced to kill it on any terms. The letter may have been a bad joke, but Nichols said he could not take a chance and not having a garden, asked if we could bury it in ours. To this I agreed but unfortunately we were overlooked in the act by Kitty, who began to weep copiously and when questioned by Louisa and her mamma could only sob that she was sorry for Uncle's Bones. It is true that she calls Nichols Uncle Charles, but we could not make any sense of the rest of it? Can you construe her meaning?

Another dismal contribution to our good doctor's sustenance was a bushel of potatoes from Nancy Newton, as a thankoffering for his delivery of her fourth infant, sire unknown. As she supplements her regular occupation by picking fruit and digging vegetables, we can only infer that the potatoes were stolen. The doctor pocketed the cash for our family account with much satisfaction, observing that doctors must live as well as w——es.

I have written you a very long letter and must now conclude with kind love to you all from Caroline, the girls and myself.

The time of which I am writing was one of the best periods of my life: my parents, my brothers and my sister were happily settled and my own family was all that my heart could wish for. My business prospered and, equally important, was a source of great interest and satisfaction to me.

It has ever been my belief that as subjects of our Creator we are bound to yield as faithful children to the laws of His kingdom. These laws do not necessarily coincide with our private interests and those which are most difficult to understand, by their very nature encourage and assist our obedience. This does not imply unthinking submission but rather a homage of the heart, acknowledging that all we have and hold is given by God. I do not believe that cruel misfortunes are sent by Him to chasten us, but I have no doubt that the minor trials of life, which form our characters, work towards His general purpose for us all. This purpose must be good, but is sometimes diverted by the folly and cruelty of man. But who am I, to analyse the Divine Purpose? 'For my thoughts are not your thoughts, neither are your ways my ways, saith the Lord.'

Truly, life is like a pair of scales where the balance is tipped first one way and then the other, and how can it fail to be so? When the balance is even, nothing occurs.

I have mentioned that my brother James succeeded so well in his printing business that he took, although not deliberately, considerable business away from his former master. This man received only his deserts, because his printing was of a low standard, at one time causing Edward, whose first book of poems he printed, much annoyance and disappointment by the numerous misprints with which the book was disfigured. Any work which in the past he had done for me had to be closely scrutinised and I was much relieved when I was able to hand all my orders to James, although if this man had been reliable I would not have deprived him of all my work.

A printer who had been a fellow-worker with James in his apprenticeship approached him for employment, informing my brother that he and his master had fallen out and had parted by mutual consent and with mutual recriminations. James knew the man to be an able workman, but could not offer him a situation as none was available at the time. He received this genuine excuse with a somewhat ill grace, although James treated him kindly and with courtesy. We afterwards heard that he had been employed as chief compositor on the printing staff of the local newspaper.

It was my custom to issue seasonal lists of my books which were circulated to the bookshops and to the county and local newspapers.

One morning, two days after the circulation of the Spring list, Mary and I were taking breakfast when we saw James hurrying up the front garden path in obvious agitation. I opened the long windows of our breakfast parlour and admitted him, breathless and flushed. 'Good God, Kit,' he exclaimed, 'have you seen the morning paper?' I reminded him that I did not see it until I reached the shop, whereupon he produced it from inside his coat and whisking over the pages, pointed to an article which according to the current custom, reproduced the book lists as forerunners to advertisements and reviews.

James pointed to a sentence, his finger trembling: 'Mr C. N. Wright's list contains a curious item,' it read, 'the book, which is described as suitable for family reading would not seem to merit this description.'

We looked at the title: by the substitution of one letter the title was made obscene.

'This is Williams's doing,' I said.

'But the sub-editor who passed the final proofs must have abetted him: otherwise there would have been no comment.'

I called on the editor that same morning and received a very half-hearted apology. 'You will please print a correction and express your regrets,' I said.

He shrugged his shoulders. 'Certainly; that is the least we can do.'

'The apology is to be in my terms: I will dictate it.'

'Just as you wish; you realise of course that this will make the matter even more absurd; by calling attention to it you will cause an even greater laugh.'

'I will take the chance.'

The apology and correction were printed and eventually the matter died down but not before we had suffered some ill-natured gibes from those of our business rivals who envied our prosperity. I was much disturbed by the whole matter, because it implied an ill-will for which (apart from the attitude of Williams) I could imagine no foundation. I was tempted to withdraw my advertising from the paper*, but knew it was inadvisable to offend the press and that whatever my private feelings might be I had no right to deprive my authors of their fair share of publicity. This decision meant my swallowing much personal pride but eventually it proved to be the right one, for I believe the editorial staff felt some confusion regarding their share in this nasty trick and our subsequent relations were amiable.

Nevertheless, this incident ruffled me because it brought home to me the unpleasant truth that every man was not my well-wisher and I accused myself of complacency. This was confirmed by a comment from Edward, to whom I had written an account of the whole matter.

'It is refreshing,' he wrote, 'to find that you are not infallible, and may I ask if it is necessary for everyone to like you? Many people dislike and envy me and I do not give a d—n for any of them. This is not vanity but humility, of which it is salutory for you to acquire your share.'

* Now extinct. Ed.

As usual, Edward's tart humour amused me and I acknowledged his good sense.

At the same time, I still did not feel comfortable in my mind and wondered with some unease if the scales were on the move again. Troubles never come singly and our next trial was a domestic one which caused some distress in our peaceful household.

Mary had engaged as a nursemaid for our children a quiet young woman who brought with her an excellent character from her previous employers. She was especially skilled in the care of infants and it did not seem strange to us that there had been an interval between her employment with the referees and her application to us, for, as she explained, she made a point of caring for babies from the month and the employment was not continuous.

She proved to be assiduous in her care of Eliza and when our dear child was six months old told us that she must soon be leaving us. 'But surely not,' protested Mary, 'Baby is so fond of you and is still so young.'

The young woman, Agnes by name, replied with some agitation that she feared she could stay for only one more week and at this point we began to speculate on the cause of her anxiety. We were not left long in doubt. That same evening there was a violent knocking on our front door, followed by a disturbance in the hall where we could hear our trusty servant, Fenton, remonstrating with the loud-voiced intruder. Instructing my wife not on any account to stir from the room, I went into the hall to find Fenton attempting to bar the way to a burly man who was furiously intoxicated and who poured forth a stream of vile language. Seeing that Fenton's efforts were ineffectual and that he was indeed in some danger, I tried to draw the man's attention to myself. In such cases a calm approach is sometimes more effective. 'Who are you, my man, and what do you want?'

'I want my wife,' he shouted, pounding one fist into the other, 'where have you —— put my wife?'

'Who is your wife?' I asked, playing for time.

It would be tedious to reproduce, even in expurgated form, the details of this man's explanation. Let it suffice that he was a travelling tinker, that Agnes was his wife, that she had run away from him, having married him immediately after she left her previous situation, that he had traced her to our house and that when he did lay hands upon her he would kill her, as he had proof that she had lived with another man and that when she had fled she had stolen all his savings.

I could see out of the corner of my eye that Fenton was attempting to slip away and summon the watch, but the infuriated man turned swiftly and pinned our servant to the wall. 'I'll get her, or I'll fire the house and kill the lot of you,' he shouted and started up the staircase, with what dread purpose we did not know, for he could not have known that Agnes was in fact upstairs. Mindful, not only of the safety of our children, but also that of the unfortunate Agnes, I got in his path and landed a blow on his jaw which had little effect except to make him reel slightly. With a bellow of rage he hit out at me, but I sidestepped him with drastic effect for I knocked over a table bearing a burning lamp which flared up and threatened to fire the wall. Fenton beat a rug over the blaze, but in the meantime the man was halfway up the stairs, at the head of which appeared Agnes, bearing in her arms a large drawer which she hurled down the stairs at her husband. Before he could recover himself, she produced another drawer which followed the first and then another, until he was buried beneath the pile of heavy drawers which she had pulled from the press on the landing.

God – and I write His name with all reverence – knows how she found the power to hurl these heavy objects, but in such moments one is given added strength. The man's yells and groans were fearsome and Fenton, who had fetched water to pour on the flames, started for the front door, but before he could reach it two of the watch stamped in from the back premises and with our help disinterred the man, battered and much subdued, and bore him away to a waiting van.

We were astonished by their appearance and it seemed, for Mary now appeared from the kitchen, that she, hearing the uproar had let herself down from the parlour window and had run for help. As we stood in the hall amid the devastation wrought by cracked balustrades, broken plaster and scorched walls and rugs, I saw as though through a mist, Agnes slowly descending the stairs, one hand at her throat, halting above the piled-up drawers. That was the last thing I remembered, through a terrible sensation of imminent death, as my heart seemed to stop.

When I became aware of myself and my surroundings again, I was in my bed, with my dear Mary sitting beside me. Suddenly all came back to me and I started violently, but Mary took my hands in hers and begged me to be tranquil, for all the trouble was over.

'The children slept through it all,' she added, smiling, 'and now you must sleep.' She gave me some physic which the doctor had left for me and told me I was to remain very quiet.

I was well again in a few days, but it was not for a long time afterwards that Mary told me how Agnes had drowned herself in a deep pool, several miles away. She was nearly seven months gone with child, which astounded us for, as Mary said, she would have defied anyone to have known, although at the time the style of dress was very concealing. The husband was dismissed with a caution after it was discovered that his story was true and that when sober he was a decent enough man. We were thankful that he was thus disposed of, for if he had been imprisoned he might have borne us a grudge.

My wife, with the strange perversity which sometimes attacks the wisest of women, shed tears over the fate of Agnes and her unborn child. I agreed that we must pity her for her faults and for her grievous end, but pointed out that she had brought her troubles upon herself. 'And please, my dear,' I concluded, 'do not quote the instance of the woman taken in adultery, because our Saviour told her to go and sin no more.'

'It is a pity the men concerned were not given the same advice,' retorted my wife, 'but I was not in any event thinking of quoting it, because every case must be judged on its own evidence. I found Agnes a very mild and good creature and I would want to know more of her history before I attach all the blame to her. She was the sort of woman who seems to attract cruel men . . .'

'There are such women,' I conceded.

'. . . and although that man was given a good character, we do not know what he was like at home. Men can be very deceitful.'

She paused, but I said nothing.

'You are a good kind husband,' continued my wife, who was sewing a child's dress and frowning a little – I hoped at her work, 'but suppose you were not, I know I could not and would not bear it!'

I know that when a woman is in a certain kind of mood she prefers any answer to none at all. 'I hope I am something more to you than just a good kind husband' I said, smiling, 'it sounds a little dull.'

'You have never loved me as you loved Diana,' said Mary, dropping her work and looking straight at me.

For a moment I was nonplussed, then I found an answer. 'Perhaps not, because I love you differently, my dear. You are the wife and dear companion of my maturity and the mother of my children.' So saying, I kissed her hand and her still fair and comely cheek. This produced a smile and the reply that sometimes she liked to tease me and that all was well.

However, I was not so sure, and I took care occasionally to voice my approval of my wife's appearance and achievements and pay her those little attentions of which it seems a woman never tires.

After this event and the sad circumstances which preceded it we seemed to draw more closely together and I was much blessed in our children, the joys of our family life and the love and solicitude of my dear wife.

And then, for the third time, tragedy broke the sacred tie and brought me to despair.

CHAPTER 10

About the time of the agitation for the Reform Bill in 1831, I and seventeen others signed an anti-reform petition, and in consequence our names were inserted in *The Nottingham Review*. The result of this was calamitous.

On the evening of Saturday, October 8, 1831, I was about to close my shop when a neighbour of mine, a Mr Drewry, dashed in exclaiming breathlessly that every pane of glass in the front of my house had been smashed by an infuriated mob. 'My wife and children!' I cried.

'They are inside the house, apparently safe. I could not get to the door, but together we might effect an entrance. Lock up here, or there will be more trouble.'

Impatient, but realising his good sense, I secured the doors and the shutters and accompanied him for the short distance to my house – on his advice, at a normal pace. 'If we run,' he said, 'they may recognise you immediately and bar our way.'

There was still a great crowd in the street, yelling and fighting among themselves, and Mr Drewry and I went to the back of the house where we pushed open the door set in the garden wall and stepped inside. Immediately, a man who had been waiting behind the door moved forward and pointed a pistol at my head. He had not, however, seen Mr Drewry who had lingered behind the door as a precaution and who, with great presence of mind, ducked around me and with his stick knocked the weapon out of the man's hand. Between us we bundled him outside and bolted the door. We then entered the house and found Mary and the children huddled together in the front parlour and unable to move because the door had been locked on the outside. Fenton and two female servants were locked in the kitchen: the third servant was missing, which proved (she never returned) that she was an accomplice to the whole affair. By good fortune the keys had been left in the locks and my wife flew to my arms, crying that the mob had threatened to fire the house. By this time I had been seen through the broken windows and a quantity of stones was hurled in on us. Bidding Mary to take the children and go with our good friend, I remained behind to collect a few necessities.

About an hour after the commencement of the attack, a squadron of Hussars, under Colonel Thackwell, came and dispersed the mob. The house was then barricaded against further assault. The relief party was just in the nick of time, as the rioters were making all preparations to fire the house.

Mr Drewry had taken my family, at my request, to the Ram Hotel, and when I arrived we were shown into a back parlour while the landlord made arrangements for our accommodation. He closed the window shutters as a precaution, but after a few minutes a fusillade of stones hit the windows and at length one of them broke a shutter fastening and a further stone knocked one of the candlesticks from the table. We were then conducted to the basement and into the wine cellar, where the children cried with fright.

Eventually all was quiet and we were taken to our rooms. The riot was over, but the consequences were serious – not only to the premises, which could be righted, but to the nervous system and the health of my dear wife. All through the crisis she had borne herself bravely, quietly reassuring the children and the female servants, but when we were installed in our room, she fainted away. After she came to herself, she made light of her condition, smiling at what she called her 'foolishness' and reproaching herself. I reassured her and comforted her as best I could for although I said nothing of it, I was feeling very ill myself and prayed earnestly that I would not disgrace myself by giving way to the importunities of my troublesome heart. My prayers on behalf of all of us were granted and in a week's time we returned to our home, to find all in order and the windows restored.

Two weeks later, I attended a sale of books at the Manor of Fiskerton. I left home at 6 a.m. by the Newark Coach and after the sale took a bed at the Waggon and Horses, Fiskerton. During the night I was very restless with a premonition of trouble. I rose at 4 a.m. and started to walk home. When I reached Culcote, I saw Mr John Howett, my assistant, driving very fast in his gig. He would have passed me if I had not shouted to him, when he cried in reply, 'I was coming to Fiskerton to fetch you: get in; Mrs Wright is very ill.'

I had left Mary with a slight influenza cold which was then epidemic in the town, but I had not had the slightest apprehension of danger when I left home. She died at about 4 o'clock on the Thursday morning. On the Wednesday, when she was still fully conscious and as always, trying to cheer me, she said – and although a truly Christian woman she seldom spoke of her faith – 'Do you know what I thought when I was alone with the children in that room and we were so frightened?'

I asked her to tell me.

'That verse in the Psalms – "What time I am afraid, I will trust in Thee".'

This was the text I had engraved beneath her name.

Thus suddenly I lost my third wife, a most good and loving woman – one of the most excellent of the earth.

The months that followed were very dreadful, for although I continued my daily life, conducted my business and my affairs in the usual way, my very soul seemed dead within me. I was forty-one years of age and although still capable of profound unhappiness, past the youthful resilience which hastens the recovery of the crushed spirit.

Moreover, although in the prime of life I was a somewhat agéd father for four children under five years of age and was worried about my responsibilities on their behalf. However, I was grateful for their existence and most fondly attached to them.

Norton, who was just over four years of age, asked me about his dear mother.

'Mamma is in heaven,' I told him, 'with our Lord Jesus.'

'I want her here,' he replied.

I was about to reprove him gently and to remind him that with Christ it was far better when suddenly, with a flash of inspiration which I truly believe was heaven-sent and intended to teach me that children need love and understanding more than preaching, I answered, 'So do I, but one day we shall see her again and in the meantime we must love each other all the more.' I took him on my knee and added, 'You are the eldest and you must help me to look after the others; especially Eliza. Always be kind to her.'

'Yes, Papa,' returned the dear child, and added after some thought, 'I am a big boy now.'

The result of this conversation was pleasing. It is true that at first Norton ordered the other children about but this caused no harm and our eldest son has indeed fulfilled our hopes and prayers.

I could not however, rid myself of a dire depression, due to my natural grief and also to a self-reproach which I did not impart to any other person. This reticence was due firstly because I did not want to draw excessively on the sensibilities of my family and friends and secondly because I knew that their attempts at consolation would be unsuccessful. So I carried my wretchedness with me and became silent and unresponsive, making an effort when I was with the children but otherwise unable to shake off my burden. Matters continued like this for nearly a year and although I knew everyone was saying how much I had changed since Mary's death, I could not help myself: even my prayers seemed of no avail.

It was Edward who finally called me to task.

I had not made a single entry in my journal for many months, but after this encounter I wrote while it was still fresh in my mind every word of our conversation and many a time through the years which followed have I referred to it.

Edward, on a visit from London and staying with brother James and his wife, entered my shop one evening as I was sorting some wrappers.

'Kit,' he began, 'I want a word with you.' His manner was such that I gave him immediate attention.

'You are going to pieces,' he said, 'and I know the reason.'

'I do not much like your tone,' I told him in the short way which had become customary with me.

'Never mind about that.' Edward seated himself on my desk and folded his arms. He was, as usual, debonair and sprightly and something of a dandy.

'You think, Kit, that it is your fault that Mary died because you signed that Anti-Reform petition.'

I was too astounded by his perception to reply.

'I know I am right,' went on Edward, 'and I am now telling you that *you* are quite wrong.'

I began to protest.

'Do not argue with me, I beg of you. For a man of your intelligence, you are behaving very stupidly. You expressed your opinion – right or wrong – and a lot of ignorant rabble objected to it. So: who is at fault? You might with better logic blame Sir Robert Peel himself for introducing the Bill. Indeed, if we traced everything back to its original cause we can blame Adam.' His tone changed and became kinder. 'Put it all behind you and start afresh. I am not a religious man, but I will wager you have asked the aid of the Almighty?'

I could only incline my head.

'And how much better off you would be if you would realise that even if you needed forgiveness – which I do not believe – God forgave you long ago and probably wonders why you continue to trouble Him.'

I was torn between my distaste for Edward's form of theology and wonder at the immense relief which flooded my mind.

'And now,' said Edward, 'have done, and be yourself.' He got off the table, took my arm and led me to a looking-glass. 'Look at me, and then look at yourself!' He pointed to the glass. 'Go to a barber and have your hair properly trimmed and tell him from me that you have the right phiz for a pair of whiskers in the new mode, cut round at the ends.* Get yourself some new clothes, for pity's sake and recover your deportment. You slouch about like an old man. You are still a handsome fellow, Kit, but you look quite run to seed.'

I told him defensively, 'I have not been well of late.'

'I am not surprised. Fretting is the worst thing for you. Do as I say and then take a holiday. We will have the children: a little London life will sharpen their wits.'

'Do you mean you will have all of them?'

'The lot: with ours, they will be a whole tribe, God help us! I shall be returning to London in a week's time. By then you must have your affairs in order, have the children ready to travel and have made a good start on those whiskers. You are fortunate: they will grow on you like grass in May.'

By this time we were both smiling, and I was feeling immeasurably better. He asked me where I would go for my holiday and I said I thought I would take a walking tour through my old haunts. Edward replied that I would do no such thing, because I needed a rest and new surroundings. I realised his good sense for the relief to my mind and spirit seemed to have brought an accompaniment of bodily fatigue. Edward recommended Brighton, saying

* mutton chops. Ed.

that the sea-air would be beneficial and that as the King was at present in residence, there would be much of interest to see.

A great bustle ensued, but by the stated time all was ready and the nurse and I took the children to meet Edward, for conveyance by the London coach. I had been surprised when he told me that he required no assistance with the children during the journey and when I ventured to ask how he would manage with Eliza, he reminded me that he had two daughters of his own and that at coaching stations there was always an obliging female to do what was necessary. He added that in fact there were obliging females everywhere and he would be very surprised if some kind lady did not come to his aid on the journey itself. 'One has only to look bewildered,' he said, laughing, 'and they all rush to the rescue. As for the lads, they will be no more trouble than so many puppies in a basket!'

I returned from my holiday much refreshed and invigorated and stayed for a week with Edward and Caroline, before returning with the children. It was a most merry household with the antics and uproar of five lively children (Miss Louisa now rising fifteen, dissociated herself from the small fry), but I must admit the little people were none the worse for their freedom. As my sister and her husband were good disciplinarians the children knew the limits to which they could go.

About six months later I was confronted with a new problem, for our excellent Susan who had taken care of the children since the departure of Agnes, announced her intention to marry. She told me it grieved her to leave her charges but her intended husband had waited patiently and for longer than he had wished and she could not in fairness defer their marriage any longer.

I reassured her and thanked her warmly for her care and for her honesty and affection. As I was leaving the nursery, she seemed about to speak, but checked herself. I asked her what was in her mind.

'Forgive me, Mr Wright, sir; but these dear children need a mother.'

I hesitated, on a wave of annoyance, then answered her calmly: 'Thank you, Susan; I think I know my duty to them.'

'You have a duty to yourself, sir, too: forgive my boldness.'

I did not reply, nor did I rebuke her. I have always tried – although with only varying success – to avoid hypocrisy, and the truth was that her suggestion, after the first shock, did not offend me in the least.

Alone that evening, I sat for a long time in deep thought, considering the matter. I knew I wanted and needed a wife. What had I to offer? On the credit side I could supply affection, loyalty and the comforts of a good home: I could even assure myself that I had by now learned how to make a woman happy. Fair enough; but what of the debits? I was forty-two years old, not robust in health, a thrice-married widower, with four children. Would the sort of woman I wanted want me?

For that matter, would any woman want to start her married life with such handicaps?

However, as always, Providence had the matter in hand, and on the following day Mr Mark Cooke, a friend of mine, called to buy some books. He was travelling to Manchester in a few days' time to purchase cotton, and asked me if I could spare the time when he returned to attend with him the sale of some turnpike gates for which he had a fancy to instal on his own estate. He was a whimsical man and could afford to indulge his tastes, but although he usually obtained that object on which he had set his heart, he was too easily apt to let his money fly. He asked me if I would bid for the gates, and although I was mystified by his enthusiasm to acquire them, I agreed to do so.

A week later, on the day before the sale, I set out early by the Dart coach and reached Tamworth at 3 o'clock in the afternoon; I then walked to Fazeley House, Mr Cooke's residence, where I was expected. Mr Cooke was out at his stables at the time but I was welcomed very kindly by Mrs Bayne, his late wife's mother, and we had a pleasant conversation. I was hoping to meet Miss Anne Cooke, my host's sister, but she was away with friends and not expected until the following day.

At tea-time we were joined by Mr Cooke, escorting four ladies, all sisters, two of whom were spinsters and two widows, who had been invited to take dinner and spend the evening. I had known these ladies some years ago and the whole company met as old friends.

We had a merry time, for two of the ladies played the pianoforte and sang very sweetly and when the music was finished, the conversation was lively and amusing. After dinner, which consisted of salmon, quarter of lamb (Mr Cooke's own raising) with a variety of delicate young vegetables; pancakes, pineapples and peaches and an excellent double Gloucester cheese, the ladies remained with us;* they to drink their wine and we our brandy.

Being intimate with my family and especially with my sister, they talked familiarly with me about the events of our youth. After we had adjourned to the drawing-room, one of the single ladies – and she the youngest and prettiest, although indeed, all were handsome – at our general request seated herself at the piano and sang a most romantic love-song, after which she addressed me, saying: 'Now, Mr Wright; if by this time you are in search of another wife, you can make an offer. There are still four of us.'

Mr Cooke, who was standing by the window, raised his eyebrows and directed at me a quizzical glance, as though to say: 'See how you can get out of this!' I did not hesitate, but immediately replied: 'There is an insuperable objection: I am so desperately in love with all of you that I cannot make a choice.'

*At this period, the ladies did not withdraw. Ed.

They all laughed heartily at my retort, saying, 'Oh, that is just an excuse' and 'You will have to think of something better than that,' etc. The pretty spinster, Miss Amelia, removed a rose from her dress, fastened it in my coat, and said, 'Put this under your pillow and see which one of us you dream of.'

When the ladies' carriage came to take them home, Mr Cooke and I kissed each one and they made a lively departure. Mrs Bayne then retired and we had a final drink before we went to our rooms. 'I wonder how serious the ladies were,' I said.

'Perhaps not at all; but who knows? Do you fancy one of them?'

I was a little confused by his question, not wishing to seen ungallant, but he said heartily, 'Come, my dear fellow, there is no need to dissemble with me.'

I then confessed that I could not imagine any one of them as my wife, adding that doubtless the ladies had merely indulged in a little harmless jocosity.

'Quite possibly, and there you can leave it,' he replied, adding, 'I am inclined towards one of them myself, but not Amelia, who in any event, has many suitors.'

Next morning we went to Tamworth Town Hall, where the toll gate trustees were assembled, with Sir Robert Peel in the chair. They were in some doubt as to the advisability of removing the gates and I told them I would be much obliged if they would allow me to make a few observations. Permission given, I pointed out that in the first place the new viaduct being finished, there would be a great reduction in the quantity of building material passing through the gates; in the next place the Dart coach would shortly be taken off the road and in the third place, the last toll-keeper had hanged himself in the wood opposite, because of the loneliness of the situation and the paucity of travellers along the road. Local gossips said that his shade appeared at night, by the gates. At this observation, Sir Robert Peel and the other trustees laughed heartily and although I could not see anything laughable about the situation, at least it served to put them in a good humour.

'Now, gentlemen,' said the chairman, 'you can make your offers.'

There were but few bidders and the offers were slow: some of the enthusiasm seemed to have departed after the hearing of my story. Eventually I topped them all by my bid and the gates were knocked down to me.

The chairman approached me. 'That was a good tale you told,' he said, smiling, 'do you always get what you want?'

I thought for a moment, then I echoed his smile. 'Fortunately, no; as to the tale, like many sad ones it is true, although I cannot vouch for the ghost.'

'That was well answered, sir,' he continued, 'may I ask your name?'

I replied, 'My name is Cash,' and produced a roll of notes amounting to two hundred pounds, which was the price we paid. Mr Cooke had previous information that the gates would not have gone for much less, as they were of a certain antiquity.

Sir Robert took the snub with a good grace, and the whole of this curious transaction being accomplished, we returned to Fazeley House to find that Miss Cooke had arrived and had retired to her room, to rest after her journey.

We were to dine at midday and I awaited the lady's appearance with mingled anxiety and excitement, for I had a strong conviction that she would be my future wife – a strange instinct, for I had not met her since she was a schoolgirl, then small and unremarkable.

When she appeared just before dinner, I knew that my instinct had been true for in the space of a few minutes my affections were fixed on her then and for ever in this life, and such powerful sensations ran through me that I could at that moment have taken her to my heart. My one anxiety was that she might be engaged to be married, but I saw no ring upon her hand and could only hope that her affections were not already appropriated.

How shall I describe her? Then in her twenty-fourth year, she was the prettiest and daintiest of creatures. Small in stature – only two inches over five feet – her excellent deportment gave her dignity. Her complexion was fine and fair, her large grey eyes with their dark, curling lashes full of light and expression, and her chestnut hair was at that time dressed in a grecian knot of glossy curls. She wore a striped rose and white gown, with a little braided jacket.

She greeted me in a manner which although friendly and gracious, did not portray any particular interest and when it was time for me to leave, my mind was in a turmoil. However, during my journey I decided that a kind Providence which had guided me all through my life would in this as in other matters care for me if I would resign myself to its wisdom.

I had received an open invitation to Fazeley House and a week later I called there, in time for tea. Miss Cooke was present as I had hoped and I could not help stealing frequent glances at her, to which glances, however, she seemed quite indifferent. Mrs Bayne chatted kindly and indeed made most of the conversation, but I must confess I was in a desperate state, wishing her elsewhere, even to the foolish extent of willing her to depart.

When the tea equipage had been cleared away, she said: 'Will you forgive me, Mr Wright, if I leave you for a few minutes, as I have some orders for the kitchen. Anne will be your hostess until I return.'

As soon as she had departed, I addressed the object of my Fond Affections, but I cannot repeat what I said, for I did not really know what I was saying at the time. I do, however, recall the coolness of her demeanour and her question, when I had faltered into silence.

'Are you making me an offer, sir?'

'Why, what else?' I asked her, in amazement, blushing very hotly and wondering what indeed my long speech could otherwise have conveyed.

'Now let us consider,' she ticked the items on her fingers,

'You are forty-two years old, you have been married three times before, you have four little children, you are rich and you believe you could make a fourth wife happy.'

'Is that how I expressed it?'

'That is the substance of your offer, sir.'

'Then I am a clumsy idiot,' I said, in all sincerity.

'You perhaps omitted something,' she suggested, with an accompanying and very sweet smile, 'no – do not come a step nearer!'

I ignored this and taking her hand in mine, made my declaration to the darling Choice of my Heart.

'Well,' she said, gently withdrawing her hand. 'I have always been told to wait for Mr Right, but I thought I would have some trifling warning of his approach.'

I begged her earnestly to consider my declaration with all seriousness, pointing out that I had been guided to her side by Providence.

'Perhaps,' she conceded, and asked me if she could be sure I wanted her for herself and not as a mother to my children. I told her that it was for herself I pleaded, but hoped she would fulfil that other gentle office.

'And if not—?'

This was a terrible question, but I answered it from my heart. 'Then I must forego my own personal joy, for I could not desert my children.'

'Bravo,' she said, laughing, but in a kind and merry manner, 'I would not have you decide otherwise. Very well, Mr Wright, I will consider your offer if you will give me due time.'

When I called two days later she was ready with her answer, which was in the affirmative.

Thus was I married to my beloved little darling Anne, and I believe never for one moment has either of us repented. I have been married to her longer than to all of my other three wives now in Heaven.

CHAPTER 11

For the first sixteen years of my marriage with Anne, my journal consisted only of routine jottings. There were various reasons for this : the ever-increasing pressure of my business; the constant and welcome demands made upon me by my children and lastly, and most significant, the satisfying and delightful companionship of my dear wife. During these years my life fell into pleasant places and if, as I think was inevitable, I sometimes looked back with sorrow on that younger self who loved with so much passion and despair, I could do so with pity for him and with gratitude for the blessings of my present existence.

From the first moment when Anne met my children and taking little Eliza in her arms, gathered the boys about her, saying with a kiss for each : 'Norton, Walter, Henry, baby, I am your mother now,' they accepted and loved one another without question or deviation, and as the years passed, the children who were so young when Mary died, would almost have forgotten the mother who bore them, if Anne had not from time to time reminded them. 'I would like them to think I was their own mother,' she told me once, 'but they must never forget her.'

I thought about this for a time and then gave her my considered view. Norton was then ten years old and Eliza seven. 'Say no more about it in future, my love; there is no fear they will not remember, and if they need to know about Mary I can tell them; so set your heart at rest. To them you are their mother.'

I believe that I was guided to say this, not the least reason being that Anne's own child had not lived to see the light and her health became frail, so that although she was no invalid, she never recovered her former strength.

The fifteenth year of our marriage was marked by one outstanding event, not pleasant to recall, but important because it changed the trend of our lives.

After an unusually severe winter and a strenuous time at business, I became suddenly very ill with influenza and was confined to my bed for several weeks. I had for some time before had pain in my left side and down my left arm and during my illness this pain became excessive. The doctor warned me that I had a long-established heart complaint which would bring me to my grave if I did not regard it seriously and lead an easier life. 'I cannot give up my business,' I protested, 'it is true that I am fifty-seven years of age, but I am not ready to retire yet.'

'If you do not give it up, it will give you up,' he said.

When I told Anne, making light of it, she said she could imagine my feelings and that I must try to take things more easily. I was grateful to her for her good sense and when I returned to business was able to do pretty much as usual, although I confess I felt very tired most of the time and had to forego my long walks with the boys – a keen deprivation.

A week or two after, Anne became very unwell. She had nursed me devotedly during my illness and her strength had been much tried. Her chest troubled her a good deal and she was slow to recover. After the doctor had visited her, she said: 'Chris, my dear, I have something to ask of you.'

I told her it was already granted.

'Dr Carlyle tells me my chest is far from strong and he advises me to get away from town and live in the country. I told him that you could not leave your business, but he urged me to tell you.'

A great fear seized me. How could I bear – or presume to take any hazards with the life of this dear one? If she were to leave me desolate, my own life would not be worth living. This was my first selfish thought: for her own dear sake she must not be exposed to any risk.

Seeing my distress and my hesitation, she said, 'It is a great deal to ask of you, my dear, but I want us to live out our lives together.'

I kissed her most tenderly. 'I shall, in the course of nature, go before you my love, but God forbid you should go before me! As for the business, I shall make Howett manager and appoint another assistant. Perhaps it will be as well if I take a rest too. I can keep in touch and make occasional visits.'

Within two months we were installed in our charming house at Fazeley, only a short distance from Anne's old home. A large garden and good fishing close at hand provided occupation for me, and there were many local activities in which to interest ourselves. When I became accustomed to our new existence, I realised that I had been very weary, also – although I felt no self-pity – that I had been working nearly all my life and it was perhaps better to withdraw while I was still not too old to adjust myself to a new life. The children enjoyed the country and Anne's health steadily improved.

It is a long time since I have mentioned my parents. At that time, in my fifty-seventh year, they were still living; my father at eighty years of age still hale in mind and body; my dear mother, aged seventy-eight, less active but in tolerably good health. After my father's retirement they moved to Church Stretton, in Shropshire, and although my father kept in fairly constant touch with my brothers, I heard from him but rarely and my information concerning my parents was derived indirectly, through them. I have tried earlier in this record to account for my father's attitude and can give no further explanation. My mother wrote to me fondly several times a year, but she was not a facile correspondent.

I was therefore much surprised to receive a letter from my father in May, 1848, saying that he had been told of my retirement and that he would like to visit me and my family and re-visit some of the scenes of bygone days. Anne and I were pleased to receive this letter and sent a cordial reply.

The young people were much interested in the prospect and I felt proud to think I could offer my father such a goodly array of grandchildren.

'Shall we line up for him?' asked twenty-year-old Norton.

Walter expressed the view that they had better be presented to their Grandpapa in instalments. 'Our combined beauty might be too much for the old gentleman,' he said.

At this point Anne reminded curly-haired Walter that he must not speak disrespectfully of his grandfather.

'Well,' said Eliza, 'he is an old gentleman, is he not?'

My wife, with her customary good humour, had to agree with our little Eliza, who in her seventeenth year was fulfilling her early promise of beauty. Fair as a lily, with her rippling corn-gold hair and her complexion like a wild rose, she resembled neither myself nor her own sainted mother but was, and indeed is, the living likeness of my own mother, the Rose of Fazeley. I have seen many pretty women in my time but have never seen a prettier little maiden than my own daughter in her first bloom, and this is not merely a father's partiality, but the solemn truth.

My father was to be escorted by a Mr Thomas Medlicott, the son of a friend of his, living in Birmingham. We offered hospitality to the young gentleman also, but this was gracefully declined in a personal letter expressing his intention to stay at a local inn and asking the name of one which could be recommended. His motive was merely to act as an escort and not to present himself as a guest.

'Mr Medlicott must be a very good-natured person,' said Anne, to which I agreed, adding, 'Should we not overrule him and invite him here?'

'I think not at first,' returned my wife, 'he does not know whether or not he will like us: let us wait and see how everything turns out.'

The family reunion was all we had hoped for. My father, who seemed to have mellowed with the years, was much affected by our hearty welcome and was greatly taken with the children, particularly with Norton, whose thoughtful and gentle nature helped to form a close tie between the generations.

My father took a walk the next morning and in no time the news was all over the village: 'Old Mr Wright is here.' A certain widow remembered his courtship of my mother and admitted that she herself knew the symptoms of a lovesick damsel when she used to see my father. 'You were a very handsome young man,' she told him. My father asked her, laughing, if he were handsome no longer to which she answered that he was not so bad for an old one.

Mr Medlicott, a personable young man of good address, made only a brief appearance at the first meeting, but at our invitation visited us on the Sunday and spent the day. It was not difficult to see that he was immediately much attracted to Eliza who hitherto, despite her charming looks, had been something of a tomboy and apparently indifferent to the company of young men. It was an experience both amusing and tender to see our daughter responding to the young man's attentions with the instinctive behaviour of her sex. For my part, as I knew she would certainly make an early marriage, and as Mr Medlicott's prospects were, as I gathered from my father, fair enough, I was content not to interfere, although I would not be prepared to consent to a very early marriage.

I discussed this with my wife who agreed that she liked Mr Medlicott, but as Eliza had so little experience of young men it might be better for her to await a wider choice.

'She has had a very wide choice ever since she has been out of the schoolroom,' I pointed out, 'but this is the first one for whom she has shown any partiality. If she falls in love with him I see no reason to discourage him.'

Anne was silent for a minute, then she said, 'I believe

you are right, my dear; but you are a most unusual father!'

I knew what she meant and had no need to comment. Fathers can be jealous of their daughters' suitors, and although I suppose this attitude can be understood, it is not admirable, particularly when it is expressed by a pretence that the young men are not good enough.

The following morning my father and I set out for Nottingham where on arrival we visited the business and toured the printing works, my father much diverted by the procedure. We stayed with James and Eliza and left Nottingham the next day at 3 o'clock, on one of the new types of train. Two gents in our carriage lost their hats by looking out of the window. They were greatly annoyed and were not appeased by my father's drawing their attention to the warning notice.

We arrived safely at Derby, but the connection was an hour after time; let us hope that at some future time trains will be punctual. While we waited we took some refreshment in the first-class rooms which were furnished in the best style of elegance, with flowering plants outside the windows, hock and champagne served in crystal glasses on tables adorned with beautiful flowers in cut-glass vases; the whole representative of what was considered the first station in England.

We continued our journey to Tamworth with first-class tickets, the fares – *5s 6d* each – being only one shilling more than the second class. It was worth the extra money, as we had a fine view of the country in all its green and luxuriant freshness and a fellow-passenger explained to us the names of the villages, the country seats and the owners' names, so that the time passed pleasantly. At a halt, about eight miles from Tamworth, a gent got out to look about him, but the train began to move off and I observed him from my window running with all his might, another gent in his carriage having hold of his hand – a most perilous situation. The running gent had a close skull cap above a long white face, presenting a most grotesque appearance, as his long coat-tails flapped and his exceptionally large boots pounded along. Finally, with a tremendous pull he was hauled into the carriage amid his own dismal cries and the infuriated shouts of a station official who did not spare his language in upbraiding the rash traveller.

We returned to home and happiness at Fazeley and took tea, after which my father rested and I went to fish with dear wife Anne at the back of Mrs Passem's (our neighbour's) garden; but the water was so low that I caught only four fish – three perch and one roach. In the evening, Mr Medlicott – now known to us as Thomas – took my father and Eliza for a drive and Anne and I walked to the church, where we left some flowers and once again studied the inscriptions. I reminded myself that in a few short years I would be numbered with the dead and asked little Anne, my own dear wife, if she ever regretted her marriage with one so much her senior. Her answer was: 'No, I could not be happier than I am; the only thing which makes me unhappy at times is the thought that you and I must part some time.'

I kissed the Dear One, for her sincerity and love, but reminded her we should be together in Heaven. She said: 'I would rather be with you now; for what about the others?'

I did not pursue this, but kissed her again and dried away her tears.

After breakfast the next day my father, I and Thomas went to Tamworth Bridge, to fish. I hooked a very large fish, supposedly a chub, but could not land it: Thomas hooked the same fish, but also could not land it. In the meantime, my father with much triumph landed a large perch. We ate our lunch – fresh rolls, which my father managed very well, having kept nearly all his teeth and in good order, cold chicken and ham, gooseberry pasties and home-brewed beer in a can from which we all had to drink in turn, the glasses having been forgotten – and contemplated the beautiful scene: rich grass meadows strewn with thousands of buttercups and numerous other flowers both simple and gaudy. The pretty yellow flag flower ever reminds me of the French dynasty, with its wars, its revolutions and its awful miseries. How sad to contemplate the wickedness of man compared with the goodness of his Creator who has placed him in a world of such surpassing loveliness. I remarked to Thomas on the evil of a nation which could slay its king, to which he replied that we had done the same thing, so we had no cause to talk.

'Two wrongs do not make a right,' I reminded him.

'And two missing kings do not condemn the whole pack,' he returned.

I did not venture to prolong the discussion, for Thomas is of a bright turn of mind and I have always been diverted by his conversation.

My father having friends at Knowle, he and I set off the next afternoon in a hired gig, arrived at 4 o'clock and put up at the Mermaid. Standing at the door was one of the friends my father sought, a Mr Cotterell, aged eighty-five. They greeted each other heartily and after he had joined us for dinner (roast beef, rhubarb pie with cream and Cheshire cheese) they had a good talk about old people and old times. Mr Cotterell's sister, a very intelligent and active little old maid, joined us later for tea. In the early evening they accompanied us to the church where we saw the tablets of our ancestors – the earliest being that of my great-grandfather, Henry Norton, born in 1684, who, if the family legends are true, led a wild and disorderly life in his youth, eventually succeeding (for he seems to have had money and some degree of charm) in winning Elizabeth Rose, a young lady of good family, who lived at Winterton Hall in the Vale of Belvoir. After marriage, he mended his ways but was convinced that his early transgressions were the cause of the family tragedies, for out of four children only one survived, all the others meeting violent deaths: one, Walter Rose Norton, by a fall from a horse; a second, William Norton, by drowning, and a third, Samuel Norton, who was an officer in the Royal Navy, by falling down the hold of a vessel.

When I had repeated this history to my friends, Miss Cotterell asked me if I believed these deaths were a sign of retribution, to which I replied that such a notion was repugnant to me and that the only direct blame which could be attached to the parents in such a matter was that they did not teach their children to look where they were going. When she smiled a little, I added, 'I assure you I am sincere: my great-grandfather repented of his youthful errors, but probably harboured a suppressed tendency towards recklessness which in its physical form he did not discourage in his children.'

There was also in the church a tablet to a young man to whom Miss Cotterell had been engaged to be married, but who was set upon by poachers when walking through his own wood, grievously wounded and left to lie all night. If he had been found earlier, no doubt his life would have been saved. I ventured to ask the lady – who must have been handsome when young – if she had not been tempted to engage her heart elsewhere, but she answered cheerfully that no-one else had come her way and she had become reconciled to her lot.

My father, with the candour of old age, at this point informed the lady that I had had four wives. Unembarrassed, but realising that Miss Cotterell would perhaps find difficulty in making a suitable comment, I said that in my opinion ladies were more self-reliant than men and were better able to sustain themselves in single bliss. Miss Cotterell rose to the occasion by saying that as eligible gentlemen were in the minority, those ladies who had not the opportunity to meet them could not be content with second best and preferred their independence. Thus the conversation was turned and when we were able later to speak privately, as I escorted her home, I told her that thanks to her, we had carried off the situation very well and with all due respect, I thought she would have made a charming wife.

'Perhaps,' she replied, 'perhaps not. In my old age I no longer think sadly about what I may have missed, but I do believe my single life has given me some patience and the appreciation of small blessings. If we cannot have the best we can make the best of what we have. Forgive me if I seem to preach: to me you seem a young man.'

As I left her at her door, I kissed her cheek and thanked her for her company.

Mr Cotterell and my father talked over their glasses and pipes until 11 o'clock, when my father and I, who were sharing a room, went to bed, but not to sleep. He told me the whole story of his courtship of my mother and when I suggested he had better go to sleep, he said, 'If I do not talk about your mother I shall not be able to sleep, for it is many years since I have been parted from her for even one night.' He then continued to talk of her good qualities and said the longer they lived together the greater became their affection and she had told him she did not want to live after him. 'How you can possibly have loved four women I do not know,' he remarked at this point. I was then so sleepy that his comment caused my mind to wander into forbidden territory: what would my life have been if I had lived it out with one of the other three – and with one in particular? By the time I had put my thoughts in order, I gathered that the old gentleman had gone to sleep.

The following morning, a lovely early Summer day, I rose soon after six o'clock and walked in the Inn garden, where – sitting in the sun – I found an old man who had fought in the Napoleonic wars. 'Them was bloody times, young gentleman,' said the old warrior. My father, who had joined us, conversed with him for some time and after bestowing a trifle upon him we proceeded to get breakfast, which was a task of some difficulty as there had been a club meeting in the Inn on the previous night and the members had not departed until 3 o'clock in the morning. Breakfast was good tea, poor ham and middling brown bread and butter, but very little of it. Charge: 1*s* 9*d* each; 3*s* each for the beds. On the whole I would call the Mermaid Inn, Knowle, a very dear house, as we had paid 3*s* 6*d* each for our dinners the previous evening, but had not minded the cost* because the food was of good quality. My father made a private joke to me, saying that he had left lying on the dressing-table a letter addressed to 'Henry Wright, Esquire' and this must have been responsible for the high prices. The title 'Esquire' had more significance in those days than it tends to have now.

We journeyed to the spot where my father was born and where his ancestors lived about 300 years ago, and where some of the happiest times of my life were spent when my brother Henry and I stayed with our grandparents, but alas, everything had changed so completely that we could no longer recognise the place. The old house had been pulled down and replaced by a new one: around it were more new houses, all with formal gardens. Gone for ever were the pond with its sweet-scented flowers growing on the verge; the fringe of common with its row of large chestnuts and stately elms; the bright golden furze where the larks and linnets nested; the nut-trees, the crab-apples and the wild damsons. The sweet song of the birds mingling with the pleasant hum of my dear old grandmother's spinning wheel formed a pleasant harmony on drowsy summer days, with the old grandfather clock solemnly marking time in the background. The shining rows of pewter plates and dishes on the oak dresser were not kept for show, as they are now, but were in daily use, the biggest dish of all most commonly used for the huge piece of bacon which was our stand-by fare. Dinner in those days was set upon the table at 11 o'clock and it was my grandmother's special pride to provide a fresh, homespun

* for current prices, multiply by seven.

linen cloth every day. The kitchen was a comfortable place with its red brick floor and white hearth, the brass warming-pans hanging above the stove and the chimney nook furnished with a well-cushioned settle. Around the walls hung eight prints of the Parable of the Prodigal Son and I asked my father where these had gone, to which he replied vaguely that he had given them away. 'I never cared for them much,' he added, 'but I suppose they may have been valuable.' He pointed out that all the fruit had gone and asked me if I remembered the delicious red gooseberries, the strawberries and the greengages. 'Everything has gone,' I said with a sigh, thinking that although all had passed away it could still be treasured in the heart's affections, only to be forgotten when the heart beats no more. For myself, I cannot visualise a heaven without flowers and trees, but perhaps I am wrong to think so.

We called at the new house and made ourselves known. Mr Allen, the owner, was not at home, but Mrs Allen and her two daughters behaved in the kindest manner, tried to answer my father's many enquiries and did all they could to give us pleasure. They made for us a bouquet from the garden and among the many flowers were some forget-me-nots, one of which I placed in my pocket-book as a remembrance of my grandmother's favourite flower. We left about noon and walked along the canal-side, past a number of locks and reached The Mermaid at about 4 o'clock, where we ordered tea – still expensive, but very good, the proprietors I think, having realised the poor quality of our breakfast. We arrived home in time for me to dress for dinner for an evening party and for Anne to give me half-an-hour to improve my waltzing.

After a week's stay, my father departed, escorted by Thomas who confessed to me that he was leaving his heart behind him and asked if he might be accepted as Eliza's suitor. I suggested that he should visit us again, in about a month's time when he would be in a better position, as our sole guest, to apply himself to his courtship, to which neither I nor my wife was averse.

'Do not speak to her before you go,' I advised, 'and in the interval she will be able to discover her sentiments towards you.' To this he agreed gracefully, in spite of the disappointment which he betrayed for a few seconds and then covered very well.

Eliza was a little quiet after his departure but soon recovered her spirits and we wondered what her feelings might be, for girls can keep their thoughts to themselves very efficiently.

The situation was made clear to us in a fortuitous fashion and by the busybody disclosure of one of our neighbours who reported to my wife that she had that day seen Eliza in the woods with young Mr Guthrie. My dear wife asked me to speak to Eliza, which I was reluctant to do, but admitted the necessity. When I questioned her she told me that she and young G. were birdsnesting. I said I did not wish her to do so again, to which she replied: 'By no means, Papa; it is a filthy occupation.'

I would not in fact have minded young Guthrie as a match for her – if she did not care for Thomas – but I doubted if he was to her taste. I had no fear that she would do anything rash, as she was both modest and sensible, qualities inherited from her own mother and cultivated by my dear Anne. I was reminded with some amusement of a friend whose daughter eloped with a young spark, but the parents did nothing, as the match was hoped for and young master and miss were much deflated as they were not pursued. Children are best managed by inculcation of Christian principles combined with commonsense and kindness.

I thought that Eliza had accepted my admonition a little too literally and went on to say that although I had confidence in her behaviour, as she was now a young lady it was somewhat indiscreet to venture alone into the woods with a young man, as it might be thought she favoured him.

'Oh,' she said, 'but I do not.'

We did not seem to be progressing. I hesitated, unwilling to put ideas into her innocent head.

My little Eliza took a scissors from her pocket, leaned out of the window and cut a bud from the roses which clustered around. This she fastened in my coat, saying, 'Now you are fine for the day. Do not fret about Harry Guthrie: I am going to marry Thomas.'

I knew Thomas would not have broken his word to me. 'But he has not asked you!'

'Not yet; but he will ask you first and you will consent will you not, dear Papa?'

'We will see,' I returned, smiling.

'That means yes,' she said, and hugged me.

We took a walk in the garden where she questioned me about my views on love and marriage, asking first if she might speak to me freely. I told her there was nothing she could not ask me.

'Then, Papa, what do you think makes a happy marriage?'

'Loving your partner better than yourself, I think. Your Mamma and your own dear mother have made me very happy and I like to think I have done the same by them.'

'And Mrs Diana?'

'I cannot speak of her.'

'I am sorry, Papa; I meant no harm.'

I told the dear child she had done no harm and that I would answer any other question freely.

'Then, Papa, I want to know what happens between a man and a woman when they are married.'

'Have you asked your Mamma?'

'The occasion has not arisen,' returned my daughter with the utmost composure, 'and I think I would rather ask you. I love Mamma dearly but you see she does not yet know I wish to marry Thomas. That is our secret, Papa. I have no other secrets from Mamma.'

Once more I hesitated. 'Supposing after all you do not marry Thomas?'

'I shall; but even if I did not, I shall marry someone, sometime. You yourself said I am now grown up.'

I had already enlightened my sons, but felt a natural reluctance to speak thus to my daughter. If, however, I did not, I would be failing her, and the knowledge had to come. God help those unfortunate wives who know nothing until the wedding night and for whom marriage begins with tears and revulsion.

When I had told her, as simply and delicately as possible, she said, 'Thank you, Papa' and sat on the rustic seat beside me for several minutes in silence. Those minutes were passed by me in some unease, but my apprehensions were groundless. 'I think,' she said at last, 'that it is quite a good plan, but I might be a little afraid of having babies.'

'Like all good things which require effort, it is worthwhile in the end,' I said.

Curiously enough, although my telling her had been for me something of an ordeal, her calm and gentle acceptance of the information convinced me beyond doubt that she was in love with Thomas. Thus most wondrously does our Creator hallow our human love and instil in us that natural desire for the mystic union of marriage.

That year we were blessed with an exceptionally fine summer. Day after day the sun shone from dawn until evening, setting in glory and rising in majesty, while the sky burned a deeper and deeper blue and the air was filled with the scent and colour of the flowers which made their gay procession through the summer months: lilies, larkspurs, pansies, stocks, pinks, marguerites and always the roses in the most brilliant profusion.

Early in July Thomas made his visit to us. I shall never forget the scene of his arrival, for all our careful plans were scattered in a moment.

In our house, the wide front door opened to a view of the back garden by means of a glass-panelled door at the opposite end of the hall. In the summer this door is left open to disclose a charming vista of the terrace with its urns of flowers, leading to the main lawn and herbacious borders. As Thomas rang the bell, Eliza was standing on the terrace, a pretty figure in her white gown, and when the front door opened she turned towards it, and with the glad cry of 'Thomas!' ran down the hall straight into his outstretched arms.

Anne and I, who were waiting to welcome him, had much ado to suppress our laughter. Fenton, who rightly considered himself as a member of the family, smiled delightedly as he relieved Thomas of his travelling bag which unavoidably was included in the embrace.

We gently detached them from each other after a short time and all of us, with arms entwined, went into the drawing room where there was much pleasant talk and laughter. After we had all taken some wine, Thomas led Eliza into the garden and Anne and I were at leisure to talk. I thought my darling little wife looked somewhat pale and I asked her if the occasion had been too much for her.

'No, my dear; I am a little overcome, though. It is the first love affair in the family and very moving. They are so much in love: how I hope they will be very happy!'

'If they are half as happy as we are, they will be most fortunate,' I said, as I put my arm around her and dried her tears.

Eliza was married to Thomas on her birthday. It was a winter wedding, but none the less fine and excellent, the church filled with guests and decorated with hothouse blooms of my own growing. Indeed, the houses were stripped, but I knew there would be plenty more by Christmas and my dear wife was very willing in her sacrifice of these treasures.

Fifty people sat down at the wedding breakfast which consisted of oyster patties; galantine of fowl, with truffles; cold pigeon pie; game sausages and tongue; cheesecakes;

ices; pineapple and peach jellies with cream, and wedding cake. The wines were Moselle and Champagne, both very good. The party was very merry and the speeches of the usual sort; some arch and witty, others sentimental and tear-provoking: all very agreeable and appropriate.

So we bid farewell to the wedded pair who departed on their honeymoon to London, the first visit to both of them. Afterwards they returned to their new house in Birmingham.

When the last guest had gone, Anne and I took ourselves to our small parlour while the feast was cleared away for the servants to partake at their leisure. They had joined the family in the drinking of healths and the eating of the wedding cake and there was enough good food left for them to enjoy an excellent meal.

'We shall miss our little Eliza' said Anne, who was sitting before the fire with her silken skirt turned up on to her lap.

I had been feeling glum on this account myself, but had tried to avoid showing it. I poured two glasses of wine and just in time, for Anne's tears were beginning to fall and she was seeking her pocket handkerchief.

'We still have each other, my love, and we have the boys' I said.

Anne put down her glass and came over. 'You have often done this for me,' she said in the most kind and loving way which yet had a hint of humour, and with her handkerchief she dried my own foolish tears.

CHAPTER 12

The year 1851 was memorable for three events: the opening on May 1 by the Queen and Prince Albert of the Great Exhibition of all Nations at the Glass Palace in London; the birth, in June, of Eliza's first child and the marriage of Norton, our eldest son, in September.

The advent of their son, Henry, was an occasion of great joy, for Thomas and Eliza had been disappointed by the tarrying of this first little one. To tell the truth, neither I nor Anne had worried over-much and had told Eliza to wait patiently, when in all good time she and her husband would be blessed. We thought that twenty-one years of age was quite young enough to become a mother and it seemed we were right, for during those waiting years Eliza learned much in the way of housewifery and had matured charmingly. She was destined to bear four more children between the years 1851 and 1863: Frank, Anne, Margaret and dear little William. All five were hearty, healthy children.

The night before Norton's marriage, Anne and I, despite our united efforts to appear cheerful before the rest of the family, confessed to each other when we were alone in our room that we felt low in spirits, knowing it was the last night that Norton (that child of many prayers) would sleep in this house where for twenty-four years he had been dutiful and affectionate in all his relationships. Although our eldest, he was the last to leave the nest, for Walter and Henry, who had both taken Holy Orders, had departed the previous year: Walter to London and Henry, after his marriage, to Birmingham. We had no favourite among our children, but Norton our firstborn held a special place in our hearts.

'Now,' I said, as we rose from our prayers, 'we must look forward to old age and the Life Eternal.'

Anne was tying the strings of her lace nightcap – a present from the bride – and did not appear to have heard me, but I was mistaken. 'You should not take that odiously cheap drink, gin and water,' she said, 'it depresses you.'

'You had some too,' I said, somewhat taken aback.

'It is a woman's drink,' she returned, illogically I thought. Then she kissed me. 'Come to bed, and do not talk nonsense.'

Norton's marriage took place at St Paul's Church, Nottingham, the home of his bride, Frances Upton (the youngest of eight daughters) whose father was a merchant in the lace trade. She looked very pretty in a blue silk gown and white feathered bonnet and the ceremony was performed by the Reverend J. Cuthbert in a manner both devotional and affecting.

There were eighty guests at the wedding breakfast which included a magnificent game pie, named in a whisper by Edward, who looked as handsome as ever, as The Poacher's Dream, and excellent wines.

The seven sisters of the bride formed her retinue and I was pleased to see that after the ceremony they were much in demand among the young gentlemen present. For a father to have seven marriageable daughters must be a great responsibility as well as a delight and I can state at this point that five of these pretty misses were destined to wed within the ensuing two years. The remaining two did not meet their destinies in the married state but are fortunately well provided for by their parents in whose declining years they are the support and comfort.

The newly-wed couple departed to the station in a carriage and a pair of greys, for their honeymoon in Scarborough.

In the evening, the Uptons held a party for the two

families and some intimate friends among whom were included a Mr and Mrs Weston and their daughter Laelia, whose looks compared very well with those of the Upton sisters. I had not seen Miss Laelia for some years and was agreeably surprised, as she had been a stout and sullen child; indeed, she did not appear too happy that evening and Anne told me afterwards that her parents were much disturbed by her attachment to Mr Con McCarthy. This Irishman, who owned a small property in the district and divided his time between it and his native haunts had a well-deserved reputation for wildness which took the forms of drinking, gambling and laying siege to the hearts – and if he had the chance, the persons – of any young woman who had the folly to listen to his blarney. He was a good-looking fellow, tall and red-haired, with a flashing smile; well-dressed but with a carelessness which betrayed his temperament: here a waistcoat buttoned awry, there a cravat tied askew. This young man professed to be in love with Laelia and had asked her father for her hand, which had been indignantly refused. Miss had then informed her parents that failing their consent she would be married without it and live in Ireland. 'I told her,' said Mrs Weston to Anne, 'that if she did it would probably be on potatoes and dripping, for I believe he has hardly a penny now, having disposed of most of his Irish property.'

We had a merry evening, with dancing in the hall – the ladies taking turns at the pianoforte, all with much skill and vigour. When we had had our fill of dancing, we played amusing games, one of which I had never heard of before. The ladies made a request that the gentlemen should visit their Menagerie in the large drawing room. Of course we agreed, and taking one gentleman at a time, two of the ladies held up a table cover before what they said was the Wild Beast, the gentleman being asked to name the wild beast he would like to see. When the cloth was lowered, only a looking-glass appeared. This caused a great laugh.

The party ended at 2 a.m. with a final toast to the

happiness of the married pair. That week was eventful, for the following day I kept an appointment with the Waterworks Committee at 1 o'clock at the Bell View Reservoir, to see the water come in from Lion Hill. I had not travelled this road for some years and was surprised to see how much it had altered. Burton Lees, a fine house, had been pulled down and converted into a brewery, excellent houses had been demolished to make a wider road, the large pool had been filled up and the romantic narrow defile with its blossoming banks and play places for the children had gone for ever. It is awe-inspiring to imagine the changes that may have taken place in a hundred years' time, when this still-busy hand is dust.

The water did not come in until 3.15 when we drank sherry and gave three cheers for the Queen. About thirty ladies and gentlemen went down below, which was lighted with candles, to drink the first glass of water. However, I declined this favour and returned home on my new horse. He had behaved perfectly on the outward journey but on the return was far from amenable, shied often at objects on the road and seemed to take matters into his own head. After a time I saw the humour of the situation and came to the conclusion, afterwards proved, that he was a joker. I let him take his course and he trotted fast, took the regular turns and got home in time for tea. I was greeted by a commotion, and found that the gardener had clipped the hedge and, on my instructions, cut down the elder tree. Hannah, our new servant, was very much put about, talking superstitious nonsense about ill-luck and that an elder tree averts evil. I reproved her, but lightly, as she was shaping to be a good servant, and as she continued to shed tears my wife intervened, saying, 'Now dry your eyes, Hannah, for remember there is a rowan tree in the front garden and that is just as good.' Hannah's tears ceased almost immediately and she departed about her duties. I told Anne that she should not encourage superstition, to which she replied, putting her arm in mine and accompanying me to the parlour, that Hannah was a country girl and believed in fairies.

'Fairies!' I exclaimed, although I could not help smiling, 'what nonsense is this?'

'I remember,' said my wife, pushing me gently on to the sofa, placing cushions behind me and taking off my boots, 'when you told fairy stories to your children and what is more, they believed them.'

'It is good for children to have pretty fancies.'

'Hannah is only thirteen years old,' said Anne, 'besides; how do you know there are not fairies? Hamlet said there are more things in Heaven and earth—'

'Hamlet was trying to get the better of Horatio' I replied, 'and was simply saying that he did not know everything.'

'Who does?' returned my wife laughing and handing me my slippers, embroidered by her own clever hands, 'now you look tired, so keep your legs up on the sofa or I shall sit on them!'

When we had taken our tea, she handed me a letter which proved to be a sadly insulting one from a Mr Campbell who repudiated a debt of £19 10s. for books. Mr Howett had tried in vain to collect the money and had eventually asked me to write.

'He says he never had them! May God forgive this wicked man as I hope to be forgiven when I am called hence.'

Anne took the letter from me. 'Now do not excite yourself, my dear,' she said, 'or you will have trouble with your heart: you are already overtired.' She read the letter and remarked. 'There must have been carelessness on our side or he would not be able to repudiate the debt. This is not the first time such a thing has happened, is it?'

I confessed that the book-keeping was not all that might be desired. 'Perhaps I should return to the business for a time.'

'That would mean living in Nottingham and you know

my chest would not stand it,' said Anne, 'why do you not put Norton in charge? His accountancy experience will be most valuable and he knows so much about the business already that he could manage it very well.'

'But will Howett not be upset?'

'Mrs Howett told me long ago that her husband worries about the responsibility and preferred his old position, but he did not wish to fail in his duty to you. Let Norton take over now and with an eye to the future and the business will still be conducted by C. N. Wright.'

When Norton returned from his honeymoon I put the proposition to him. He agreed willingly and I made the business over to him altogether. This worked very well indeed as he still consulted me, but I had no worries or responsibilities and the financial situation was very sound there being, by the grace of God, plenty for all of us, with something to spare for those less fortunate, named by Anne as her 'cottage friends'.

The winter that year was a hard one with little snow, but continual and piercing winds. Soon after Christmas Anne suffered a severe cold and kept to her room for several days, afterwards not venturing out of doors for three weeks. I was worried about her and called on Dr Neale to ask him if he had any fears regarding my wife. He reassured me and said that with care she would live for many years. He then enquired of myself and after examination told me that my heart was no better; neither (thank God) was it worse and with this I was content.

On behalf of several small commissions entrusted to me by Anne, which included flowers for the church altar, I called upon the vicar, the Rev. James Cuthbert, and found him entertaining Mr Con McCarthy who looked, Heaven help him, wilder than ever. I offered immediately to withdraw but the Irishman departed in a greatcoat which looked several sizes too large for him. I remarked on this to Mr Cuthbert who said, 'It belonged to his coachman: I fear he is in a sad way.' Quite properly he made no further comments and I could not ask questions. He was, in any event, more interested in imparting the news that on Sunday we would be visited by the Rev. Dr Bell, who would preach the morning sermon. I had heard Dr Bell before and thought his style both recondite and verbose, but the majority – particularly the ladies, who doted on his looks and his rich voice – admired him greatly.

His sermon on the Sunday morning, which lasted for one and a quarter hours, was a learned doctrinal discourse on the Mystery of Atonement, to some extent marred by the bad behaviour of one of the choirboys. Anne was not at church and I had felt some reluctance in leaving her with Hannah, the girl being too young and I feared, too silly to be trusted. Some young ones try hard and others appear to be senseless. When I returned, to find all was well and told Anne of my fears, she advised me to be indulgent, reminding me of my own youth and adding that when young herself she was a foolish creature, her own father having told her, although not without playfulness, that she was mindless. This I could not imagine about my darling little wife.

'As for choirboys,' she said, 'I know the one you mean: he is a very little boy and I am sure finds it hard to sit still during a sermon. I find it very difficult myself sometimes. I am sorry I missed Dr Bell; I like to listen to him even if I do not understand all he says.'

On my birthday, the 6th March, we discovered some crocus out in the garden, also some almond blossom which we picked to decorate the house. Anne was much better and although it was a rimey day the sun shone brilliantly and we were both in good spirits for we were expecting Eliza and Thomas and little Henry. They arrived in time for early dinner which was roast sirloin and Yorkshire pudding, cauliflower and roast potatoes, with apple pie and cheese and sherry trifle for the ladies. Thomas and Eliza were both well, and baby in his velvet frock and white pinafore very pretty and gay. Norton and Fanny joined us at tea-time, looking very cheerful, as indeed they might, in expectation of a happy event.

The conversation, a genial uproar as at most family gatherings, punctuated with the alternate coos and cries of Henry intent on squeezing his bread and butter between his fingers, turned on the subject of names. 'If we have a son,' said Norton, 'I suppose he will be Christopher Norton.'

Eliza asked if they could not choose an alternative, otherwise there would be much confusion. I was reminded of the occasion when Norton was first called by his name and cried bitterly, imagining in his infant mind that he was being called naughty. This reminiscence was received with much laughter by the company, for of such pleasant inanities are family jokes composed.

'Reverting to your own child,' I said, 'by all means make a change, but we must have a Norton at some time or another. All I ask is that you do not leave it too late.'

My wife and I retired in excellent spirits after a very happy day and rose the next morning in the light of brilliant sunshine and unclouded blue skies. Anne stood at the open window enjoying the fresh breeze. 'Spring has really come, I think,' she said, 'but I never feel it is really here until I see the daffodils. I cannot understand how Shakespeare, who lived only about fifty miles from here, could speak of daffodils in March, but perhaps it was warmer in those days.'

We took our breakfast in the small parlour which opened on the terrace, a pleasant room on sunny mornings. On the walls of this room hung the portrait of my other three wives and Anne made a pleasant remark. 'Diana looks happy this morning.' I glanced, but only for a moment, at Diana's lovely face and then laid my hand on Anne's. 'And you look happy too, my love; you do not mind the portraits any more?'

'Truthfully, Chris, I seldom notice them now. You know how one gets accustomed to things.'

Anne's own portrait, well-painted by an accomplished artist, hung in the drawing-room. I prayed at that moment that I would never see it join the others, selfishly hoping that I would die first.

We had finished our breakfast and were taking a walk in the garden when Hannah sought us out crying, 'Oh, sir; oh ma'am; Mrs Weston is in the parlour asking for both of you and she is in a great taking!'

We were by that time used to Hannah, who in spite of her want of manner was a good servant in many ways, so we merely dismissed her and returned to the house, not too disturbed, for Mrs Weston was a lady inclined to exciting herself over trifles. However, we found her in tears and great distress, scarcely able to speak: indeed her sobs and lamentations became so unbridled that at Anne's bidding I poured a glass of wine for her. 'Now,' said my wife, 'drink this, dear Mrs Weston and try to tell us what has happened.'

At length we extracted the story, which was cause enough for woe. Laelia, who persisted in her infatuation for Mr McCarthy, had taken a walk in the woods early that morning and had seen him 'with' – here she blushed deeply, one Nancy, daughter of the corn-chandler (a very pretty girl, by the way). They were too much engaged to see Laelia, and speeding back to her home, she took her father's shot-gun, returned to the woods and discharged it at Mr McCarthy, but her aim being poor, succeeded only in peppering one of his legs. This she did not know at the time and seeing him roll over, doubtless with shock, imagined she had killed him. Dropping the gun on the ground she fled back to the house and reported the proceedings with sobs and cries.

Hastening to the spot alone (Mr Weston was away on business) Mrs Weston found no trace of Mr McCarthy or Nancy, from which she concluded that he was still alive.

'Where is Laelia?' asked Anne.

'I have locked her in her room, the sad wicked girl. Her father can deal with her later.'

'You do not want this matter spread abroad,' I said, 'I advise you to return home and release Miss Laelia who I warrant will stay quietly enough at home for the present, and I will seek Mr McCarthy and see what is to do.'

Anne said she would accompany Mrs Weston and we all set out on our different ways. I found Mr McCarthy, as I anticipated, in his cottage, with Mr Bird the surgeon attending him. He gave me a very meaning look and said he had had an accident while in the woods, no doubt from the gun of a poacher, who had disappeared after the accident.

The surgeon departed, saying he would return later in the day lest a fever should arise, and when we were alone Con McCarthy asked me, 'And on whose behalf are you here?' Before I could answer, he went on, 'I know who shot me – that little fool Laelia. That gun has her father's initials burnt on the barrel.'

I told him that I knew the story and that I had in the first instance called to reassure all concerned that he was not seriously injured. 'No thanks to her,' he said, 'you can take the gun back and tell her that I have done with her.'

'Did you not make her an offer?' I asked, in some indignation.

His answer was to laugh in his rudest manner and to remind me that his offer had been refused. 'I do not live in the past,' he said, 'and I give my favours where I choose. A girl like Nancy has some sense and does not think that every bit of fun leads to the altar.'

'But how many of these girls have you spoiled for honest husbands?' I asked him sternly.

'None of them, thanks be to God,' he answered with shocking flippancy, 'I'm not like some who leave a trail of bastards behind me. I know too much.' He gave another of his loud laughs. I decided to say no more, as it was not my business and to speak the truth I thought that in spite of his wounded leg he looked dangerous. However, he suddenly changed his tone and said, 'Come, I have no quarrel with you and I take it kindly that you sought me out. I have no interest in pursuing this matter for the mischief is done but I will tell you for your ears alone that I am engaged to a young lady in Ireland and shall soon be marrying her. And now sir, you may take the gun and go.'

I departed and returned to the Weston's house. Laelia was seated in the drawing-room with her mother, her cheeks very white and her eyes very red. I gave a brief account of the interview, suppressing much of it, and concluded by advising Mrs Weston to keep her husband in ignorance of the whole affair.

'Can I deceive him?' she asked me.

'You are not deceiving him. Of what use would it be to tell him? And you, Miss Laelia, if you will accept advice from one old enough to be your grandfather, I suggest you forget the matter and be thankful it is no worse.'

Laelia was contemplating her folded hands and without looking up, said in a very low and bitter tone: 'It was a stupid thing to do; but I shall not forget and one day I shall find a way to punish him.'

I countered her mother's cry of protest by my suggestion that Laelia was still suffering from shock and had spoken at random.

When I reached home Anne questioned me and to my surprise blamed everyone but Con McCarthy. 'He made an offer for Laelia and it was refused.'

'But his conduct with Nancy?'

'I do not wish to be uncharitable,' said my wife, 'but by this time Nancy knows quite well what she is doing. If Mr McCarthy is truly engaged to the young lady in Ireland, he probably misses female society.'

'This is strange morality, coming from you my dear.'

'I am not speaking of morality, but of facts. It is useless to pretend that men do not act like this or that girls like

Nancy do not encourage them, but in any event it is not Laelia's business!'

There seemed nothing more to say, so I tried to end the conversation with a joke. 'It is said that all women like rakes.'

'And all men are jealous of them!' My wife put on an offended air.

I did not reply to this, but after a few minutes I told her that we seemed to have quarrelled, but I was not sure what the matter was about. She laughed then, my little darling Anne, and told me that all was well between us, and to think no more of Con and his problems, for I had done my best. I was much relieved by this, for I do not like to make Anne cross.

The next stage of this affair was that Laelia did after all marry Con McCarthy who, it seemed, after all was rich, his earlier pretensions to poverty having been a part of the general eccentricity of his conduct. He had told no-one but myself of the lady in Ireland and I kept the secret, believing him at the time; indeed, I was inclined to accept it as truth when after the shooting incident he was absent in Ireland for several weeks and I assumed that he had ended his engagement with the Irish lady. I was not surprised that he and Laelia married, for undoubtedly she had a passion for him and he had cared enough for her to offer marriage, her worldly parents not withholding their consent when they knew he was rich.

McCarthy bought a property only a few miles from our district where he installed himself and his wife in luxury and became very exclusive, consorting only with the best families: he could when he liked, assume a grand air and was well connected. Their child, which appeared seven months after their marriage, was accepted as premature by everyone. If we had our doubts, we said nothing.

Their story should end here, in this commonplace manner, but its true conclusion was a strange one. After two years, the McCarthys left the district and went to live in Italy. A friend of my brother James, who was a newspaper reporter chanced to comment on the McCarthys' departure and told James that when he had visited Ireland, nearly three years previously, he had read a newspaper report which, as it concerned someone of local interest, he had followed up by visiting the district concerned. There had truly been a lady to whom Con McCarthy was betrothed: it was she who was very rich, but she was his senior by ten years or so and was not attractive. The lady lived near one of the great lakes and was much addicted to boating. During McCarthy's last visit they went on the lake together, a sudden storm blew up, the boat overturned and she was drowned. He was a strong swimmer but vowed he was unable to save her as she hampered his efforts by nearly dragging him down and she was large and well-built. Some suspicion attached to him but nothing could be proved and he inherited her fortune.

When Anne and I discussed it between ourselves, she said: 'I did not dislike Con McCarthy, but I think he would be capable of anything. I believe Laelia is a match for him, for she was a very stubborn and unbiddable child and I do not think she has changed.'

Yet two more years later, Con died in Italy of a stomach affection and Laelia returned, a rich widow, without encumbrances, for her child died in infancy. She never remarried but lived quietly in her luxurious house, retained all her old friends and engaged herself in charity and good works.

After Laelia had returned from Italy, Anne took me in the garden and when we were well away from the house, said, 'Do you think Laelia poisoned Con?'

'You mean because she said one day she would punish him? No; I think it was a judgment upon him – that is to say if he was responsible for the other poor woman's death.'

'And if not,' said Anne with a sigh, 'it was just sad ill-fortune for everyone concerned.'

'The ways of Providence are beyond the scope of our limited understanding.'

My wife put her hand in mine. 'Providence does not seem to be practical at times. Would it not have been easier to prevent Con in the first place – that is, if he did do it?'

'Let us assume he did not; in charity we should not judge.'

'But that almost makes it worse: all so sad and unnecessary. What do you really think, Chris?'

I did not answer for some time and then but hesitantly. 'I think that all good things – which we are inclined to take for granted – come from God and all bad things from the Devil. God could stop all evil at its source, but if He did this would not be earth, but Heaven.'

'You really do believe in the Devil?'

'Certainly I do. He is named Lucifer and rebelled against the Creator. Even atheists, may God help them in their last extremities, recognise the existence of both good and evil. In the last war before the Day of Judgment, Lucifer and his Legions will be overthrown: in the meantime they continue to defile the world.'

'Is this theology?' asked Anne, wonderingly, 'if so I understand it better than Dr Bell's.'

'It is not theology,' I said, smiling, 'but the reasoning of a plain man. I am no paragon, like Dr Bell.'

CHAPTER 13

In the year 1864, we left our large house and took a pleasant small one with a fair-sized garden. Fenton had retired on a pension and we needed only one maidservant – our faithful and affectionate Hannah, now efficient in all things – and a boy, to assist in our smaller quarters. Anne welcomed the relief from the cares of a large house as she sometimes suffered sadly from neuralgia in her head and her spine, painful and at times almost disabling. It grieved me very much to see my dear wife suffering pain, but I am thankful to say that between the visitations of this affliction she was well enough and could follow her usual occupations.

The business continued to prosper and I made occasional visits to the shop where it was agreeable to see the improvements from time to time, such as the installation of the new gas lighting very bright and fine; to meet old friends and new customers and above all to see and handle the new books. And while I am on this subject, may I beg those of my dear readers who have borne with me thus far to employ the utmost care with new books while they are still in the shop. Do not open a book more than an inch or so for perusal, as if it is opened widely it loses its symmetry. When you have made your purchase and the book is yours, you may do as you please.

I had a long-standing invitation to visit Caroline and Edward who were then living in Norwich and Norton suggested that while I was there I might transact some business in cases where a personal visit would be desirable. The arrangements were in hand for my journey, but were postponed for a short time by a letter from Thomas, asking if we would take care of little Willie for a few days as he had had a severe cold and needed a change of air. Anne suggested that if possible I should delay my Norwich visit as she knew I enjoyed the company of our grandchildren and she liked to share it with me.

Thomas arrived with Willie two days later. We had not seen him for ten months and now, at four years old, he was a very beautiful and engaging child with russet-coloured curls and the deepest blue eyes I have ever seen – the hue erroneously described as violet. He cried a little when his Papa left him but soon recovered and sat on a little stool in the garden, watching me get up a row of potatoes. After a supper of bread and milk and brown sugar, he repeated his prayers and kissed me goodnight. 'Goodnight and God bless you, Willie,' I said. He took Anne's hand and pulled it. 'May I whisper, grandmamma?' he asked her.

Anne bent down and inclined her ear. When he had whispered, she said aloud, 'Yes, I promise you. Now upstairs to bed, William.'

When she returned to the room, smiling, I asked her what he had said. 'He wishes to be called William,' she replied, 'so I promised. He wants to please you and says he can repeat the twenty-third Psalm.'

'That is more than I could do when I was his age,' I said, 'we will hear the dear child tomorrow.'

The following day, after breakfast, William repeated the Psalm correctly and with touching expression. For this he received kisses and half-a-crown for his money box. We spent the morning in the garden where he ate a plum and then an apple, which at first he did not like. In the afternoon, while Anne rested indoors, we sat in the summerhouse where I told him of his dear great-grandmother, now in Heaven.

Anne and I both thought the roses were already returning to his cheeks but were greatly shocked when he was taken ill in the night with sickness and fever. We sent for Dr Higginbotham who asked us what he had been eating and when we told him said the fruit had undoubtedly caused the trouble and that we should have known better. Anne and I were much distressed as William was still very poorly and still in a fever the next day, despite the doctor's physic. Hannah then intervened, saying she had seen her young brother in such a condition and the best remedy was an infusion of sage leaves, which with our permission she would prepare. Thinking that at least this could do no harm, we allowed her to concoct the mixture and whether or not this worked the cure, by the same evening our little boy was better and by the next day was quite well.

We invited Norton and Fanny to make a little party for William by bringing their children to tea. John and Norton were very good and well-behaved, but little Janey, the youngest, was a very bad child – the most passionate little thing I ever did see: we made sure we would not have her again until she had improved.*

In July, 1870, I made what I decided would be the last of my many trips to London. On the first morning of my arrival I visited Walter and his wife at Kensington, then walked to Charing Cross then to the Thames Embankment, to look at the Houses of Parliament and the river, which view as ever gratified and delighted me. I then walked to the office of Longman, to see Mr Reader, afterwards to Lockwood and Company and finally to call on Mr Miles of Simpkin Marshall.

After luncheon at the Britannia Hotel, Newgate, I called on my nephew George, of the firm of Corbin, Wright and Company, wholesale chemists, who greeted me with affection and took me to a small and select inn where we shared some excellent iced punch. After making more business calls I returned to the Britannia and took tea with Mr Whitaker, Publisher, Author, and Proprietor of Whitaker's Almanack. During our conversation, I mentioned some of my recollections of the London of nearly

*she became a well-known actress when she grew up. Ed.

seventy years ago, when I arrived with only one shilling in my pocket. Mr Whitaker said I should set them down and when I confessed I had indeed done so and had written a record of my life, he suggested that *Chambers Journal* might publish it, as he knew the editor who he was sure would be interested.

'It would need editing,' I said somewhat ruefully, 'but perhaps my son Norton will do this.'

'Have it done,' said Mr Whitaker, 'and we will see to it.'

I mentioned this to Norton when I returned home and he said he would do this, so perhaps in a few years' time when I am called to rest, the work will be done.

I then made my way by omnibus to Edward – back in Chelsea – to spend the week-end. Our dear Caroline had died only two years since and although Edward missed her sadly he was endeavouring to make the best of the remainder of his days. He was aided in this by the kindly and faithful services of his housekeeper, a Mrs Warren, who had entered the household forty years previously, as a young widow.

After a hearty welcome from him, I asked him how he did, and he said he was well enough. 'I am not a religious man, Kit, as you know, but I believe that true love never dies and that is immortality.'

As Edward had been explaining to me all his life that he was not a religious man, and as I had always found him one of the kindest and best, his protests did not worry me overmuch. To do myself justice (and who does not try to do this, however little justice he affords to others?) I have never tried to convert anyone to religion. Children must be brought up in the faith and if later on they choose to reject it, their parents have not failed in their first duty. Those who rear children in ignorance of the faith, saying that later on they can choose their own path, are wanting in good sense, for how can they select, when they have no knowledge of the alternative?

'You are silent,' said Edward.

'I was thinking: we are told that God is Love.'

It was Edward's turn to fall silent. Then at last he said, 'I take your point, old friend. Perhaps there is something in it after all.'

We then talked of other matters. It was a pleasant, balmy evening and we sat in Edward's library with the windows open on to the garden, a small plot mellow-walled, the borders thick with flowers and the lawn as excellent a piece of turf as I have ever seen. This house, to which he moved after Caroline's death, is very small, but perfect and beautifully-appointed. We had had our dinner of lamb cutlets and peas, followed by cheese and a little fruit, and were enjoying our wine, a very palatable port, one of ten dozen laid down at the christening of Edward's youngest grandson, Charles Southgate, twenty years ago.

'You have not changed much with the years,' I told him.

'Our old friends never grow old,' said Edward, laughing, 'but my youthful portrait over yonder contradicts your kindly assessment.'

I glanced at the picture. 'I was not referring to your appearance,' I said, 'although I think you have matured very well, like this excellent port, and like me you have kept your hair and teeth. I meant rather that you have not aged in your manner or your speech like some old fogies – including myself, I suspect.'

Edward laughed again and told me not to fish for compliments. This amused me very well and we continued our conversation, not dwelling much on past affairs, although a certain amount of reminiscence was inevitable, but discussing current affairs, he with a liveliness which elevated my spirits.

'The port reminds me,' he said, 'that I have a pleasant meeting in store for us all. Charles is coming to luncheon tomorrow as he very much wants to see his great-uncle and you have not seen him since he was a schoolboy.'

I knew that Charles was reading law and I was much interested in his progress. By this time our family had grown to a prodigious size and I had sixteen grandchildren and numerous nephews and nieces of the first and second generation. It was (and is) the pleasant task of Anne and myself to remember all their birthdays and until the age of twelve years, all receive half-a-crown, which is increased to five shillings as they enter their teens. As he or she reaches majority, a handsome gift is dispatched, after which they have to shift for themselves until they marry, when we start afresh. This gives us pleasure and keeps us in touch with our descendants.

Charles had grown to be a good-looking young fellow with a quiet and somewhat sedate manner well suited to his intended profession. On Sunday afternoon we took a walk by the river which looked very beautiful with the sun making diamonds on the ripples and all of us were content to enjoy our surroundings without much talk. Later, when we had taken tea in the garden, I asked Charles about his work and received lucid answers: I told him I thought he would do very well, as he could express himself clearly and concisely.

'I believe I shall master the technicalities in time,' he said, 'but I think it is also very important to understand other people.'

'You should read Immanuel Kant and Aristotle,' said Edward with apparent gravity. I made a guess at his thoughts which I believed coincided with mine: that only time and experience can give insight into other people's characters and that there is no short cut to this branch of wisdom.

Charles, poor youth, looked somewhat taken aback. 'I do not know Kant but I have attempted to read Aristotle and find him rather tedious.'

Edward pretended to look shocked but I would have none of it and confessed that I found Aristotle a great bore and that in any event, his discussions applied more to self-examination and self-discipline than to the understanding of others.

Edward had not finished with his teasing. 'Kant deals with metaphysics, the process of thought and the origin of being: this might enable you to disentangle the mysteries of another person's soul.'

Poor Charles looked more dismayed than ever.

'And how much of this did you understand, may I ask?' I challenged Edward, to which he replied laughing that he had gained his knowledge of people by studying them first-hand and that although no two people were alike, there were recognisable types.

'But how will this help me?' asked Charles.

'You will have the advantage of knowing your client's past history and his record of behaviour: these will indicate his category and people almost invariably behave in a manner true to their type.'

'But,' said Charles, 'supposing a man in all other respects honest, tells just one lie – which may be all-important in evidence – how could it be detected?'

'There is no such thing as one lie,' replied Edward, 'it resembles the greenfly: married, bedded and the parent of innumerable offspring before it can turn around.'

'There is always some sense in your nonsense,' I said to Edward, 'and to it I would add this, Charles: a man hitherto honest, who has made one slip, will soon give himself away: beware of the malefactor who looks you straight in the face!'

On Sunday morning I attended Chelsea Old Church where I was much impressed by the singing, the devotional conduct of the service and the excellent sermon by the incumbent, the Rev. W. H. Davies. In the afternoon we drove to Hyde Park and had much ado to make our way for the agglomeration of carriages which were drawn up to witness the driving past of some foreign potentate who was on a visit to our gracious Queen. Fortunately we were able to extricate ourselves before we were too much hindered at our rear and much enjoyed our stroll among the trees in the lush beauty of their early summer foliage.

We took tea with my nephew (by marriage) Herbert Spencer who allowed us ten minutes' conversation by his watch and then departed to his study, leaving us to finish our tea and enjoy the excellent madeira cake, to which we did full justice. We were shown out by the servant who informed us civilly that his master was engaged and hoped we would excuse him. We took this good-humouredly enough and Edward said to me afterwards that he hoped Herbert's books sold well; for his part he was quite unable to read them.

We returned home, having enjoyed our outing, and I asked Edward if he still played the pianoforte on which dear Caroline had been such an excellent performer. 'I have not touched it since she left me,' he said, 'although it has been tuned regularly. I have not had the heart.'

'Play to me now,' I asked him, 'music is a great solace and when you have taken the first step you will be able to play some of the tunes she loved.'

'Can one still play when one is so old?' he said, but even as he spoke he was unlocking the piano and raising the lid. He played well and thus we passed a pleasant hour, afterwards taking our supper in the garden: cold chicken with some early asparagus, strawberries and cream and a very good hock. Our coffee was made in the Turkish style which Edward was very anxious for me to sample: I found it rather unpleasant, but did not tell him so.

I went home next day by a fast train (sixty miles an hour and most comfortable) not knowing that Edward and I would never meet again in this world. In the autumn of that same year he took a sudden chill which turned to congestion of the lungs, an illness from which a sufferer of advanced years has little chance of recovery. His death was a great sorrow to us.

*   *   *

It is now late August and after a lovely day spent mostly in the garden with my beloved Anne, I am seated at my desk in the lamplight, writing these last words. There is nothing left for me to say and some other pen will write 'The End' to my life story. I leave no great fortune but am rich in family affection and have enough of worldly goods to ensure the comfort of my dear ones, resigning myself in thankfulness to Him who is the Founder of all things.

I offer up a prayer of gratitude to Almighty God in whose mercy I have so long lived, and so with joy I look unto Him who is our Creator and Preserver.